MW01228892

A Life in Paragraphs

A Life in

Robert

Introduction by Ian Brown

Paragraphs

Fulford

Essays

Optimum

A Life In Paragraphs
© Ottawa, 2020, Optimum Publishing International and Robert Fulford

First Edition

Published by Optimum Publishing International
a division of JF Moore Lithographers Inc.

All rights reserved. No part of this publication may be reproduced in any
form or by any means whatsoever or stored in a data base without
permission in writing from the publisher, except by a reviewer who may
quote passages of customary brevity in review.

LIBRARY AND ARCHIVES CANADA CATALOGUING IN PUBLICATION
Fulford, Robert, 1932
A Life in Paragraphs, Robert Fulford

ISBN: 978-0-88890-303-7

Digital Version of the book is also available ISBN: 978-0-88890-304-4

1. A Life in Paragraphs.   I. Title

Cover and text design by Bryan Gee
Cover Illustration by Seth

Printed and bound in Canada

For information on rights or any submissions please write to:

Optimum Publishing International
144 Rochester Avenue
Toronto, Ontario,
Canada. M42 1P1

Dean Baxendale, President

www.optimumpublishinginternational.com
Twitter @opibooks

This book is for Geraldine Sherman, my wife.
She willed it, and then she worked hard to make it a reality.
Every writer should have such a loving partner.

CONTENTS

Paragraphing

¶	Begin a paragraph
no ¶ / run in	No paragraph. Run in or run on
[2] ¶	Indent the number of em quads shown
flush ¶	No paragraph indention
hang in	Hanging indention. This style should have all lines after the first marked for the desired indention

Punctuation

⊙	Period or "full point." Periods and commas ALWAYS go inside quotes
,/	Comma — ⊙ or :/ Colon
;/	Semicolon
’	Apostrophe or 'single quote' "pos"
“/”	Quotation marks "quotes"
?/	Question mark or "query"
!/	Exclamation point or "bang!"
-/ or =/	Hyphen — $\frac{1}{en}$ or en En dash
$\frac{1}{em}$ or ⊢⊣	One-em dash — $\frac{2}{em}$ Two-em dash
(/)	Parentheses (parens; curves; fingernails)
[/]	Brackets (crotchets) — } Brace

Miscellaneous

e/	Correct letter or word marked
e/⊗ k/⊗ or X	Replace broken or imperfect type
9	Reverse (upside-down type or cut)
⊥	Push down space or lead that prints
(SP)	Spell out (20 (gr)) (Also used conversely)
(G?)	Question of grammar
(F?)	Question of fact
(2 y au:) or (?)	Query to author (2u?)
(2y Ed)	Query to editor (2u Ed) A ring around a marginal correction indicates that it is not the typesetter's error. All queries should be ringed
OK w/c or OK a/c	OK "with corrections" or "as corrected" — Correct and print; no revised proof wanted
⌐	Mark-off or break; start new line
End	End of copy: # or 30 or End

solid	Means "
leaded	Addition
lead	Insert le
ℊ ld	Take ou
⁀	Close up
(#)	Close up
✓ or ‿	Less sp
eq #	Equalize
thin #	Thin spa
l/s	L E T T E R
#	Insert sp
space out	More spa
en quad	½-em (n
□	Em quad
□□□	Insert nu

Insertio

OUT see copy	Insert ma (Mark
the/l	Insert ma
ℊ	Dele—ta
	Delete a
stet	Let it sta

Diacritical Ma

ü	Diaeresis
é	Accent ac
ô	Circumfle
ç	Cedilla o
ñ	Tilde (Sp
use lig	Use ligatu
/	Virgule; s
*	Asterisk
⁂	Asterism
⊙□⊙□⊙	Ellipsis .
	Order of

Introduction

One quality I especially admire about Robert Fulford's essays –apart from their calm erudition, the certainty of their judgment, and the boggling range of subjects he wraps his mind around (everything from television to the tango, from H. G Wells's sexual affairs to parataxis in the King James Bible) – is that each one feels securely packaged. Adequate wrapping is a rare quality in prose at the best of times, especially these days on social media, but it's deeply welcome here: you never have any anxiety, reading Bob Fulford's essays, that the string around one is going to come untied and fly apart mid-journey, leaving the logic of its argument and the language of its expression strewn across the landscape like something that fell off the back of a truck.

This is because Fulford, in addition to being a hugely gifted writer and thinker and reporter and reader in the classic journalistic tradition, also happens to be one of the best and most reliable editors Canada ever had. If you didn't know this before you read *A Life in Paragraphs*, you would know it five pages in. Fulford is what A.J. Liebling, another panoptic reporter who could write beautifully and deeply and fast about anything (he was one of Fulford's early heroes), would have called "a careful writer." It was Liebling's highest compliment, and it describes Bob Fulford to a T.

It is also a standard Fulford passed along to any number of younger journalists he has edited. I suspect most of them can remember the first time their stories were worked over by Bob Fulford, during the two decades he was editor of *Saturday Night* magazine and publishing the most ground-breaking journalism in the country. I certainly do. The experience is scalded into my permanent memory the way one's first close shave with complete disaster tends to stick in mind, causing shudders decades later.

I was 23. I had been a reporter at the *Financial Post* and at *Maclean's*, and I was pretty sure I knew everything there was to know about writing. But I had never written for magazines, which in those days were where all the best writers appeared. I had been assigned by Bob to write a story about the crippling Inco strikes in Sudbury, Ontario, in the late 1970s, and had delivered my story when, two days later, Bob called and asked me to come in for an edit.

I was shown into an office by his assistant, an amusing young woman. Fulford was sitting at a long table and told me to take the chair next to him. I had not imagined magazine editing was so intimate.

My story lay in a neat pile of typewritten pages in front of Bob. It didn't seem to have a mark on it. "It's a good story," Bob said, "It just needs some tightening."

He then proceeded, for the next forty minutes or so, to tighten the story in front of me, in ink, on the page, as we flipped through it. He used classic *Chicago Manual of Style* copy-editing symbols, and made sure I could see what he was doing. It was like watching Raphael repair the work of a keen but inexperienced assistant: a few deft brushstrokes instantly elevated the entire painting into a previously unknown realm of accomplishment. He cut words and sentences and even paragraphs. He'd say, "This is unclear, what do you mean?" Every time I used the word "it," he forced me to make it concrete; every time I used "that" he took it out. I felt like someone who had had the cerebellar equivalent of a colonoscopy that, while no anesthetic was used, was nevertheless painless due to the skill of the surgeon.

At last, we arrived at the concluding sentence of the story. I had spent the length of the piece amassing evidence of how poorly both the company and the unions had served the lives of Inco's employees, but felt compelled to come down on the side of labour, because that is what I thought I was supposed to conclude. Bob cut the last half of the last line, changing it to say that neither the unions nor the company had served the workers well, thereby restoring what I had actually discovered.

He did this in front of me, never hesitating, never going back, never erasing a single mark. It was as if he had the purer version of the story memorized in his head, and he was cutting through to that essence.

But what amazed me most of all was the way he seemed to understand the story as a physical entity, as a weight of facts and sentences and paragraphs in the form of pages. We had to carve the story out of that block. This act of engineering was going to try to take up actual space in the attention span of readers, so it had to be worthy of the spot. We just had to find the right shape, its inevitable outline, in the blob I handed in.

I kept that Fulford edit in a file, and re-studied it every time I wrote a story for at least the next five years. I still have it, and I still look at it. Making those marks on the page in front of me, Fulford changed the way I thought about writing. I thought writing was something one did in the mind. Fulford taught me – and anyone who ever watched him type on two fingers at 150 miles per hour on his upright manual will understand this – that good writing is also physical, that it has a physical presence. You can literally feel good sentences. It is something writers do in their brains within their bodies, which then translates into the story's body. This made writing – especially good writing, precise and well-crafted writing – that much more rewarding to study and learn from.

Judging from the immense erudition and confident range and exemplary clarity of these essays, that is how Bob Fulford has written for the past 70 (seventy!) years – observing, then writing, then rewriting, then reaching deeper into his reading and reporting and knowledge to craft a bigger and sharper truth. No matter how intimidating his subject – Freud, Emperor Julian, and post-modern academic writing are just three of the snarling dogs he takes on – Fulford is never intimidated. He reads, he reports, he thinks, he types. He eschews opinions, preferring to write to figure out what he thinks, as he points out in his essay on the writer and thinker Walter Benjamin: "the first-class reporter accumulates facts until, properly sorted, they turn into knowledge." In Fulford's hands, the process often then moves to the level of illumination. Again and again, I found he had written about a subject I wished I'd written about: he has an unerring eye for important stories, with the result that A Life in Paragraphs often reads like a sprightly trot through the cultural highlights of the Western world from the Second World War to the present day. And yet he never chooses the hot take or the obvious story: he avoids what Allan Bloom, one of his favourite subjects, referred to as "the tyranny of the present."

Fulford does this by doing what so few of his fellow journalists have managed: he writes only about what he really wants to write about. "Writing for me usually involves pleasure," Fulford declared in 2011, at the age of 79, shortly after suffering a small stroke. That pleasure is evident everywhere in these essays. He's now 88, and he's still writing. He keeps going, he tells us, "because of curiosity, the reigning impulse of my life, the source of my happiness." The day will inevitably come, sadly, when the endlessly inquisitive cultural cornucopia known as Robert Fulford is no longer writing. That day hasn't arrived yet.

IAN BROWN

Preface

Journalism is my job, my craft and my passion. At age 88 I realize that I've never stopped reading magazines and never wanted to. Articles are my lifeblood.

When I was growing up I began paying close attention to the magazines brought home by my father, an editor at the Canadian Press. He liked *Time*, and I can still remember him saying that *Time*'s obituary on Franklin Roosevelt in 1945 was so good that he became lost in it while reading on the streetcar. He overshot his stop by nearly a mile and ended up a half-hour late for supper. I was 13 that year, impressed by his shrewd judgement, perhaps anxious to emulate him.

I too liked *Time*, and kept reading it till it turned into just another tired advertising vehicle. By then it had played a role in my education by its detailed coverage of architecture; it was the only newsstand magazine that showed a serious interest in that subject, and I was grateful.

In the middle of my adolescence my uncle bought me a subscription to the *New Yorker* at Christmas. Since then I've never willingly missed an issue. I became an addict of A. J. Liebling, a *New Yorker* star. Through his writing I learned a great deal about war, sports, newspapers, France – and prose. First editions of Liebling books sit today on a shelf in my office, for frequent re-reading. When jazz became a major interest for me, I began reading *DownBeat*, the jazz magazine, for which I later wrote.

Over the years my close attention to journalists delivered the best part of my education. George Orwell instructed me on the evils of totalitarian communism and the devious emptiness of everyday political rhetoric. Jane Jacobs celebrated the virtues of street life in old-fashioned neighbourhoods and saw, before anyone else, the sterility of the housing "projects" that planners and architects spread across North America. James Baldwin took his readers, who included me, into the darkness of bitter, frustrated Afro-Americans who were treated as a permanent lower class. Each of these teachers (for that's how they functioned) had a message for their readers. Some writers stumbled into the great story of their lives, as Jacobs did when she innocently accepted an editor's request that she cover the housing projects – then recoiled at what she found.

Others, like Baldwin, started with a colossal grievance and found the language to express it. In all cases, they wanted to be heard.

But while each of these mentors leaves me with enormous gratitude and unending pleasure, they leave untouched a major shortcoming of contemporary life: The sameness of almost everything built around us – roads, schools, buildings, theatres, suburbs.

Life is abundant and at the best times personally satisfying, but it is lived in a world designed for efficiency and little else. Monotony, blandness, drabness: This what we build for ourselves and what we are apparently fated to go on building. In this environment our humanity is unfulfilled and the human imagination, the spirit of originality, is forgotten.

Two German philosophers, living in the United States in the 1940s as Jewish refugees from German dictatorship, produced a theory that explains both the persistent tone of 21st-century North America and the many places where that tone is imitated.

Theodor W. Adorno and Max Horkheimer, members of the Frankfurt School, together wrote *Dialectic of Enlightenment: Philosophical Fragments* (1944). It was a modest title covering some challenging ideas. They used the term "dialectic" because it was a favourite word of Marxists (which they both were) and they mentioned the Enlightenment because it describes a moment of history in which much that we cherish first established its importance. The Enlightenment was the great era of promise in science, art, and human rights.

Reason was high on the Enlightenment's list of qualities. It was developed as an "emancipatory" quality, a way of opposing an oppressive church and the rights of kings who inherited their power. But Enlightenment reason could be used otherwise, and was – by fascism especially, but also by corporations and governments.

Adorno and Horkheimer coined the term "culture industry," comparing culture in a capitalist society to a factory producing standardized cultural goods, such as films, broadcasting, and magazines. Homogenized, these products tend to manipulate mass society into passivity.

Another philosopher, Emmanuel Lévinas, wrote of "instrumental reason," the use of reason as an instrument for determining the most efficient means to achieve a given end. Through its embrace of instrumental reason, Western philosophy displays (he thought) a destructive "will to domination," which suggests it was responsible for the major crises of European history, particularly totalitarianism.

Certainly instrumental reason created the sameness that now burdens us. We are now accustomed to the fact that branded chains and standardized architecture make our cities more boring than they should be. Take a trip from Baltimore to Vancouver and you sense that restaurants and clothing stores all seem to be created by the same tired designer who created the highways and condo buildings. It was no surprise recently when Starbucks opened its biggest-ever coffee shop with one bar 88 feet long – in Shanghai.

Philip Roth was once asked why he wrote. He answered that it was his way to be freed from his own narrow perspective on life and "to be lured into imaginative sympathy with a fully developed narrative point of view not my own." The pieces in this book arise from a similar impulse, to free myself from routine ways of thought.

To that end I pursue the tango to Buenos Aires, search for the meaning of the Talmud, study the myths of Robertson Davies, immerse myself in the pleasures of the movies, and contemplate Grey Owl, the greatest fraud in Canadian history. These are all pleasures, but at the same time they are ways of teaching myself, broadening my knowledge and the knowledge of my readers, as the Enlightenment recommends.

The Wayward Course
of Memory

In the autumn of 1945, at the age of 13, I saw a star-encrusted MGM comedy, *Week-End at the Waldorf*, with Ginger Rogers, Lana Turner, and Van Johnson. It was filmed in glossy black and white, with what I later learned to call "MGM lighting," a style that bleached out even the distant possibility of nuance.

The producers set out to make a featherweight parody of *Grand Hotel*, the famous 1932 Greta Garbo film about several interlocking dramas unfolding in a Berlin hotel. In *Week-End at the Waldorf* MGM proudly displayed a collection of famous names, like a countess exhibiting her jewels. In the hotel Van Johnson, back from the war, is falling in love with Lana Turner, a stenographer named Bunny. Walter Pidgeon is a famous war correspondent, Keenan Wynn a junior reporter. Robert Benchley plays a columnist, a kind of narrator. It was an agreeable film but in my view certainly not memorable. On that last point, I was dead wrong.

Twenty-five years passed. My oldest children, then 12 and 10, wanted to be taken to a movie, and I noticed that *Week-End at the Waldorf* was running at a revival house. In my mind it was amusing but unthreatening, the two qualities a father desires in entertainment for the young. After the usual negotiation, which included a clause on popcorn and soft drinks, we settled on my choice.

Watching it, I was astounded by the details I remembered. I knew the ending of certain scenes as soon as they began, as if I had seen them the day before. The old war correspondent was annoyed when the junior reporter awakened him by knocking on his hotel room door. As the door opened, I knew the camera would pull back so that we could see the correspondent had posted on his door a sign saying "do not disturb" in eight or 10 languages. He asked the reporter whether he was a linguist and then ran through the various languages on the sign.

After a while I stopped telling the children what was coming next. They weren't at all impressed, no doubt because they had no idea what 25 years meant.

Forty more years passed. Turner Movie Classics showed *Week-End at the Waldorf* on television, and I stumbled across it while looking for something else. I watched for half an hour and still could predict each scene.

This experience, not at all unusual in my life, demonstrates
the most perverse and arbitrary quality of memory, its mad and
maddening unpredictability. We might consider it natural if people
retained scenes from movies they cared about – if I, for instance,
more or less memorized Ford's *Stagecoach* or Hitchcock's *North by
Northwest*. That would make a kind of sense. But *Week-End at the
Waldorf*? Hardly.

The standard texts describe the hippocampus as the part of the
brain "where memory is organized." But not, I suggest, organized
well. Whatever happens in this process has none of the reliable quality associated with a librarian's word like "organized." Fickle, volatile,
erratic – those are appropriate adjectives. Memory emerges from
the hippocampus like telegraphed news dispatches in the American
Civil War, when both Union and Confederate armies made a habit of
snipping the wires of the other side, so that bulletins from the front
often arrived in fragments.

To make the hippocampus bulletins even less credible, they pass
through a totalitarian system of censorship. Unconsciously we try to
obliterate whatever data might be dangerous and therefore should be
treated as confidential: ask any psychoanalyst, or for that matter any
wife or husband.

History also offers a parallel to this form of secrecy. During the
First World War the officials of the Kaiser's Germany thought it best
for morale if they withheld bad news of the fighting and reported
only the victories of their soldiers. So German civilians believed they
were winning until early in November 1918, when the news broke
that they had suddenly, inexplicably, lost. Their actions in later decades suggest that this ugly surprise drove them mad.

Our conscious minds, calling up transmissions from memory,
have no means of recognizing the distortions created along the
way. What makes it worse is that these fragmentary accounts of our
personal history often enter consciousness when we least expect
them, and often when they are least welcome. Embarrassments of
the distant past, which we have "long forgotten" – cruel words said
in anger, for example – are suddenly unearthed in the cluttered files
of the hippocampus and speedily reported. There must be no one on

earth who has never been betrayed by this randomly triggered intracranial version of the Freedom of Information Act.

"Memory," says Cees Nooteboom, the Dutch novelist, "is like a dog that lies down where it pleases."

I'm in my eighties, an age when you are entitled to free prescription drugs and portentous thoughts about the future. Naturally, I brood about memory. I had a stroke in 2008, the mild kind that my neurologist classified as "lucky." But, stroke or no stroke, memory often weakens in the old; for one thing the brain is shrinking. So in recent years I have noticed curious gaps in what the hippocampus was reporting.

By now I'm used to recently acquired words and names making surprising and unaccountable disappearances. The term "word-finding" describes the system by which the right word at the right time appears to those with still sharp memories. Some old people learn an antonym, word-losing: Words long known and never neglected, not obscure words at all, suddenly are found to be AWOL. I've worried ever since I somehow lost the word "treadmill." Again and again, I reached for it and discovered that it wasn't in my accessible vocabulary, where it had been living for decades. Logically, this might betray a dislike for exercising on the treadmill; I might have unconsciously jettisoned "treadmill" out of disdain or boredom. That might make emotional sense. In fact, I enjoy my half an hour daily on the treadmill; it gives me a chance to watch Turner Classic Movies. Even so, it could be that I harbour a deeply unconscious dislike for any kind of exercise but don't care to acknowledge it. Or, possibly, the hippocampus just doesn't give a damn, one way or the other.

Only someone in his ninth decade could understand that I'm glad I can still call up the $20 prize I won in late adolescence from the CBC'S *Jazz Unlimited* program. It was for an essay on the theme "my favourite record." I chose "Four Brothers," a Woody Herman record, and I can bring back the four saxophone players whose solos gave the tune its name: three tenors, Stan Getz, Zoot Sims, and Herbie Steward, and a baritone, Serge Chaloff. The prize came in the form of a gift certificate from a record store. I bought a Billie Holiday album, which included her version of "Yesterdays."

That's one of the thousands of bits of memory that remain with me. But perhaps I won't have it forever. Slowly, I hope very slowly, memory is bidding me goodbye. The signs are clear. Odd facts vanish without explanation or apology. Testing myself a few years after my stroke, I tried to list without hesitation the 12 prime ministers who had governed in my lifetime, starting with Harper, going back to R.B. Bennett. Swiftly I scored eleven, but I flunked out on Kim Campbell. A few years earlier I would have had all 12.

I am good with long-term memory, not so good at short-term. That can be a bother, but it has compensations. If you are 80 or so you must have, in the nature of things, more dead friends than living ones. The people older than you are mostly dead and so are many people your age. The past is not a place to dwell, but it always repays contemplating. I can remember, for instance, a couple of dozen older colleagues, men and women who ushered me into my profession, helping to turn a timorous and not terribly swift journalist into a happy and productive craftsman. I like to remember the young *Globe and Mail* reporters, all of them in their twenties, who tried to instruct me in my late adolescence. They found my gaucheries not appalling but forgivable. They were followed by a platoon or so of editors who took me by the hand and steered me in something approximating the right direction. They are now installed (fairly securely, I hope) in the long-term division of the hippocampus.

I can call these people back from the grave, listen to them, maybe continue arguments we had long ago. I have lost many, many contemporaries, victims of drink or exhaustion or just bad luck. I miss them, and miss especially our youthful times together. With memory's help I'm glad to invite them back when they are needed and glad to welcome them when they make unscheduled visits.

It is only when your once-proud memory weakens that you begin to know memory's importance and its mysterious nature. A memory that comes to you exists in time but not space. It has no weight, no dimensions, no sound, no colour, no texture. Yet it is a fact, often a significant one. In any case it's as much a part of a human as a finger or an aorta. It is as real as the brain that creates it.

Memory is to an individual what a library is to a city and what the World Wide Web is to twenty-first-century civilization. It holds my history and establishes my place in civilization by charting my myths and my principles. It contains my mistakes and my satisfactions. The daily lives of all of us are governed by the mazes of technology, commerce, and culture, but we rely on our memory-stored traditions to guide us through them. It's only by consulting what the past taught us that we can even begin to understand the present. Kierkegaard expressed a central truth when he said that "Life is lived forward but is understood backward."

Memory is a box that more or less automatically fills in the course of a lifetime. Everything goes in, from T. S. Eliot to high school romance, from childhood misery and the joys of maturity to the neon lights of Tokyo, from *The Tempest* to "Mairzy doats and dozy doats and liddle lamzy divey," a song that clogged the airways in 1943, entered my unprotected brain and has not yet had the grace to go the way of "treadmill." No one can catalogue the contents of the box, and probably that's just as well – many of us, perhaps all of us, would be ashamed of the chaos revealed in our reservoir.

What we all fear most, those who are climbing the upper rungs of demography, is the day when the box empties. We rarely discuss that event; the thought of it is too hard to keep in mind for more than a moment. When forgetting is the subject, I prefer to be amused by my favourite confession of memory failure, delivered by Lord Palmerston, the nineteenth-century British prime minister and foreign secretary, when he was asked about a major European issue of his day, the long-running territorial dispute between Denmark and Germany:

"The Schleswig-Holstein question is so complicated, only three men in Europe have ever understood it. One was Prince Albert, who is dead. The second was a German professor who became mad. I am the third and I have forgotten all about it."

Surprised by Love: Chekhov and "The Lady with the Dog"

DETAIL OF THE PAINTING EXEMPLARY BEHAVIOR BY HORATIO HENRY COULDERY (BRITISH, 1832–1893)

Coughing up blood so often that he carried around a small private spittoon, Anton Chekhov slipped into the last stages of TB and then died at a sanatorium in the Black Forest town of Badenweiler. He was ridiculously young, just 44, but what now seems absurd about his death is the date, July 15, 1904. A century has passed since he died, yet he remains close to us – his stories never out of print, his plays often in production and frequently quarried for movie scripts (two films of *Uncle Vanya* alone in the last decade), and his sensibility in the air around us at every moment. He's the supreme modernist in drama and fiction, omnipresent like no other writer.

On the one-hundredth anniversary of Chekhov's death, I happened to pick up the August 2004 issue of *Toronto Life* magazine and found myself reading an eloquently Chekhovian story, "Leo fell," by David Bergen. It takes place in the present in two extremely unChekhovian places, Kenora and Winnipeg, but it's melancholy like Chekhov, funny like Chekhov, and tough like Chekhov. And it ends in precisely the way that Chekhov invented and impressed upon the world.

Those who knew Chekhov did not guess that their doctor friend was to be the father of both the modern theatre and the modern short story, but they knew they were dealing with someone exceptional. When Maxim Gorky read Chekhov's "The Lady with the Dog" in the December 1899 issue of the journal *Russian Thought*, he wrote to the author: "You are doing a great thing with your stories, arousing in people a feeling of disgust with their sleepy, half-dead existence ..."

Gorky's words suggest how variously Chekhov can be read. No one today makes a point of expressing disgust at the people depicted in "The Lady with the Dog." On the contrary, we are more likely to notice Chekhov's great-heartedness and the generous treatment of his characters. For Gorky it was natural to consider them symbols of decadent old Russia and to see Chekhov as a potential supporter of the new politics. Gorky's name, which he chose, means "The Bitter." He was on his way to becoming the founder of Soviet socialist realism, driving Russian literature down a blind alley. Chekhov, on the other hand, was striding onto the bright plains of modernity, shaping a literature without limits.

Since then people of every political and intellectual opinion have found reasons to quicken as they read Chekhov or see him performed. Vladimir Nabokov, who of course hated everything about Gorky, loved Chekhov and loved in particular "The Lady with the Dog." Long ago, James T. Farrell remarked that the translation of Chekhov early in the twentieth century was a turning point for English-language writers, the signal to revolt against the conventional plot story and draw closer to the true rhythms of life. In the early 1980s a New York editor asked 53 of the leading short story writers of the world, from Updike and Gallant to Kundera and Borges, what writers had most influenced them. The writer most often cited was Chekhov, a result that will surprise no careful reader of the fiction written in the last century.

The story that Gorky admired so much has come into English under various titles – "The Lady with the Dog," "The Lady with the Pet Dog," "A Lady with a Dog," "Lady with Lapdog," and "The Lady with the Little Dog." The dog walks into the first sentence, accompanying Anna, a married woman who has come to Yalta by herself from a small provincial city, as she strolls the seaside promenade. Gurov, a banker from Moscow, also alone, seduces her, as he has seduced many women before.

Gurov does not look back on these conquests with affection. In fact, he has discovered that when he loses interest in a woman she becomes hateful to him. As always, Chekhov makes this point with a telling detail, which appears in English in several versions. In different translations Chekhov can be more or less subtle, more or less cruel. The Chekhovian tone persists, but translators inevitably inflect it in different ways.

Consider the way Gurov's sour dislike of the women he has known fixes on their underwear. In 1919 the first great translator of the Russian writers, Constance Garnett, rendered a certain passage this way: "When Gurov grew cold to them their beauty excited his hatred, and the lace on their linen seemed to him like scales."

The original text contains just one word, *chesuya* (scales), mentioning no creature to which the scales belong. Translators have felt free to elaborate on it in order to convey the revulsion Gurov feels. In 1964 David Magarshack translated the passage as: "the lace trimmings on their negligees looked to him then like the scales of a snake." In the 1970s

Ronald Hingley rendered it as: "the lace on their underclothes had looked like lizard's scales." And in 1991 David Helwig put it: "the lace on their underwear became the scales of a reptile." Thus the imagery varies – first scales, then a snake, next a lizard, finally an unnamed reptile. All versions make the point, some with more graphic intensity than others. We who do not read Russian can only guess at the overtones Chekhov wanted us to hear in that single word.

Gurov expects the encounter with Anna to be as brief and casual as his earlier affairs, and the story turns on his surprised recognition that something more significant has happened to him. When he and Anna return from Yalta to their separate home towns and families, he discovers he cannot forget her. She has entered him in some way; she is with him all the time. She's like a safety net (to borrow a simile from the early Alice Munro) that's stretched beneath him; he never knows when he's going to fall into it. He goes to her town, risks a scandal to speak with her, and obtains her agreement to meet him in Moscow. They are in love, yet they can see no way to be permanently together. Eventually they discover that this clandestine love has become their reality, and their lives with their families are now only shadows, meaningless but impossible to escape.

The nineteenth-century feelings running through a Chekhov story like this one could as easily be emotions of the twenty-first century. Beneath his narrative we sense a profound personal investment in love, much like the one most of us still make or long to make. Without quite articulating our purposes, or examining them, we pour into the vessel of love many of the emotions and expectations once connected to religion; at the same time we look to romance and marriage for a concentrated version of the satisfactions once provided by expansive family connections.

Chekhov understood that sexuality, when partially freed from traditional constraints, soon provided its own intricate set of problems. Gurov's customary attitude to lovemaking demonstrates an affliction that often accompanies liberated sexuality, an aversion to intimacy. In even the most sensitive among us this may well appear as cold-blooded opportunism. It may also lead us into seeing sex as the way to solve the puzzle of a relationship; in this frame of mind you "get it out of your system," purging yourself of a feeling by physically expressing it. In Gurov's case, as in many others, the lovers find instead that unwanted bonds between them have been silently, almost secretly created.

Chekhov characters tend to be trapped: by their marriages, their parents, the rules of their communities, their own lassitude, or the very nature of Russia. They yearn to escape. In Chekhov, yearning is a major theme, like manliness in Hemingway or anger in Philip Roth. Chekhov's people yearn for a different life, one they can just dimly imagine. In the course of a story they often discover that their present existence seems false. They see the truth, announce that they must change, and usually discover that they cannot escape. Bernard Shaw said that Chekhov's genius lay in discovering that for some characters the tragedy is that they do not shoot themselves.

Chekhov bestowed on the writers who came after a magnificent gift: he demonstrated that not every issue raised in a serious work of fiction has to be resolved. Some, in fact, are better left unresolved. He did not believe in what we now (unfortunately, and misleadingly) call "closure." At the end of *Uncle Vanya* we are told explicitly that the dreary provincial frustration we have observed is all that his characters can ever know. Who could have guessed that, a century after the first performance, audiences would demand to see this story enacted again and again? Not Chekhov. He wasn't sure it worked in the first place.

Among its many distinctions, "The Lady with the Dog" is, I believe, the only short story to which a book of criticism has been devoted. In 1973 Virginia Llewellyn Smith, in *Anton Chekhov and the Lady with the Dog*, argued that no other work of his better expresses Chekhov's attitude to women and love. In its twenty or so pages, he draws together so many threads of thought and experience that the story becomes a summary of all that he will ever know about the subject.

In 1899, at the age of 39, Chekhov fell in love for the first time. He set his heart on Olga Knipper, an actress eleven years younger. He had been tubercular for some time, and to save his diseased lungs from the Moscow winters he was spending months of each year in what he called "abominable Yalta," the drowsy resort town on the Black Sea. He felt like an exile in the south, but he had no choice. Every autumn, as the first cold winds arrived in Moscow, he would begin coughing blood.

He had a fresh reason for disliking Yalta in 1899. Olga was not there. Earlier in the year they had grown close, and he had slowly come to understand the depth of his feeling for her. Now she was gone, back to her work in the theatre, and he was alone. Boredom afflicted him at the best of times, and now he had to deal with both loneliness and boredom. It was in this state that he wrote, in August 1899, "The Lady with the Dog."

Is the story an account of their love? No – and yes. It is not about them because, first, Gurov is a banker rather than a doctor and writer, Anna a housewife rather than an actress. Both have spouses and children back home, so their affair must be secret. Chekhov and Olga Knipper were not married, and though they were discreet they had no need to hide their meetings.

Adultery was not an issue in their lives, and in the story adultery is far from incidental. It takes place, and was written, during a long moment in the history of sensibility that we might call the golden age of adultery, the era that began in 1857 with *Madame Bovary*. A certain kind of "modern adultery" was providing a rich vein of drama and comedy for literature. As an act of love adultery retained the weight of meaning that it would begin to lose in the middle of the twentieth century. The newly emergent bourgeois of Russia placed family at the centre of their concerns. Lifelong marriage vows were embraced with deep seriousness, which made the frisson of sin and fear more intense than it has been for earlier or later generations.

At the same time, changes in social life provided increasing opportunities for breaking those vows. Women were moving toward independence, which might even take the form of holidays on their own. Railroads made it easier for lovers to meet. Anonymous hotels were everywhere. For the prosperous, living a double life was increasingly possible. Like many writers, Chekhov was delighted to exploit the narrative possibilities offered by this new world of erotic mystery and danger.

The experienced Gurov and the innocent Anna see adultery in sharply different ways. After they make love for the first time, Gurov remains aloof. He is satisfied, but she is disturbed. She says, "It's wrong. You will be the first to despise me now." Gurov doesn't bother to reassure her. There's a watermelon on the table. He cuts himself a slice and begins to eat.

And then, Chekhov writes, "There followed at least half an hour of silence." That's an astonishing amount of silence, an eternity in a situation of this kind, and every time I come across it I think for a moment that it's a mistake. It's not. Chekhov is saying that Anna is paralyzed by shame and cannot articulate her distress. And Gurov has nothing to say to her. Finally Anna begins: "God forgive me. It's awful.... I am a bad, low woman; I despise myself and don't attempt to justify myself."

And then, as if this titanic sexual act has somehow cracked open her personality, she confesses to Gurov her feelings about her life:

> It's not my husband but myself I have deceived. And not only just now; I have been deceiving myself for a long time. My husband may be a good, honest man, but he is a flunkey! ... I was twenty when I was married to him. ... I wanted something better. ... I wanted to live! To live, to live! ... I was fired by curiosity ... I told my husband I was ill, and came here ... and now I have become a vulgar, contemptible woman whom anyone may despise.

And the next paragraph begins: "Gurov felt bored already, listening to her ..." But she goes on: "I love a pure, honest life, and sin is loathsome to me. I don't know what I am doing. Simple people say: 'The Evil One has beguiled me.' And I may say of myself now that the Evil One has beguiled me."

This scene makes clear why Chekhov has arranged for his lovers to be married. Adultery is not the theme of his story, but adultery charges it with tragedy and guilt. That's why adultery filled so many pages of nineteenth-century literature. It was an event that a woman like Anna could regard as an earthquake in her life.

All of these details distinguish Gurov and Anna from Chekhov and Olga. But the similarities and parallels are equally striking. Gurov, like Chekhov at that time, must be satisfied with occasional moments of love, intermittent and limited, snatched from the demands of their other lives. More important, Gurov's responses to Anna echo Chekhov's to Olga. Chekhov's friends found him loveable and admirable, but a student of his life often encounters references to his detached attitude to women. Like Gurov, Chekhov needed the company of women; by comparison, men bored him. And yet – again like Gurov – he found their emotions hard to deal with and preferred to keep his distance.

In the language of this period we might say he found it hard "to commit." He kept marriage at bay. Ronald Hingley in his biography says Chekhov required his female friends to "be beautiful, elegant, well-dressed, intelligent, witty, and amusing; and above all that they should keep their distance." Another biographer, Philip Callow, author of *Chekhov: The Hidden Ground* (1998), writes: "In a feminine part of himself he was drawn to the unpredictability of women, yet their emotional crises threatened his independence and he feared their intrusion into his inner life. The barrier behind which he lived held firm until the arrival of Olga."

There was a secret self he had guarded with care. Now he discovered that Olga had not only penetrated this self, she had become part of it; and this is precisely what happens to Gurov. Chekhov was writing the story in August with Olga on his mind. On September 3 he wrote her the earliest of his love letters that survives: "Dear, remarkable actress, wonderful woman ... I've become so used to you that now I feel lonely and simply can't reconcile myself to the thought of not seeing you again until the spring."

Chekhov at that moment hadn't reached his fortieth birthday, but he knew that tuberculosis had aged him. He transfers this perception of age to Gurov, who is also just under 40. At the end of the story Gurov, in a hotel room to meet Anna, glances in a mirror and sees himself as old and ugly: "And it was only now, when his hair had turned grey, that he had fallen in love properly, in the way that one should do – for the first time in his life."

"The Lady with the Dog" makes a clear point. What Chekhov says in this sophisticated parable is that love radically alters the landscape of existence. When touched by love, we know the world in a different way. Love changes the inner landscape, too. Under the pressure of love, Gurov looks inside himself and sees someone he has not known before, someone capable of feelings that he barely knew existed.

In the Soviet era Russian commentators used to say that Gurov was regenerated by love, made into a better person. Love had become a moral force. Those critics were not entirely wrong. In fact, Chekhov originally wrote at the end that love "made them [the lovers] both better." But he deleted that idea. He didn't want to dictate a moral. As a thought it lacks the tact we expect from Chekhov; it presumes too much.

The ending he used instead has become a legend. Writing when Chekhov was still something of a novelty in England, Virginia Woolf said that at first he baffles the reader. "A man falls in love with a married woman, and they part and meet, and in the end are left talking about their position and by what means they can be free ..." And Woolf quoted from the ending, the thought that "the solution would be found and then a new and splendid life would begin." She wrote: "That is the end. But is it the end? ... it is as if a tune had stopped short without the expected chords to close it." Does that make it inconclusive? No, she decided. With an alert sense of literature we will hear the tune, and in particular the last notes that complete the harmony.

Many others have been fascinated by the ending, but the most surprising treatment of it that I've seen appears in a biography unrelated to Chekhov. In 1968, by some strange means, the closing passage of "The Lady with the Dog" migrated from Chekhov's work over to Michael Holroyd's biography of Lytton Strachey, where it appears, undisguised but uncredited.

The closing sentence in the Constance Garnett translation of Chekhov reads: "And it seemed as though in a little while the solution would be found, and then a new and splendid life would begin; and it was clear to both of them that they had still a long, long road before them, and that the most complicated and difficult part of it was only just beginning." Now consider a passage from *Lytton Strachey: The Years of Achievement, Volume 2*, by Holroyd. It's 1917 and Dora Carrington has fallen in love with Strachey; she has learned for the first and last time what it is to love, and Strachey as a homosexual cannot physically return her love. This is how Holroyd ends that chapter: "... it seemed as though in a little while a solution must be found, and then a new and wonderful life would begin. And it was clear to her that the end was nowhere yet in sight, and that the most tortuous and difficult part of it was only just beginning."

One of my readers, Doris Cowan, pointed me to the Holroyd passage. I thought of writing to ask him how Chekhov's conclusion ended up in his book. I decided finally that I'd prefer to speculate. My guess is that, like many people, Holroyd read "The Lady with the Dog" many times, and read the ending with special care, because of its place in literary history as well as for the pleasure it gives. Eventually the words became a part of him and he innocently placed them inside his own text, where they fit perfectly.

Nabokov was perhaps the most distinguished of all the critics who wrote on that ending: "All the traditional rules ... have been broken in this wonderful short story.... no problem, no regular climax, no point at the end. And it is one of the greatest stories ever written." He gave six reasons why it was great, the sixth of which was: "the story does not really end."

In not ending it opens onto other stories; it leaves us with an infinity of possible results; it describes lives in process rather than lives completed. This is the sort of ending that serious short story writers around the world have ever since laboured to achieve. It is the kind of ending now familiar to the readers of Katherine Mansfield and Morley Callaghan, Flannery O'Connor and Tobias Wolf, a score of *New Yorker* writers, and many more authors, all of them in some way Chekhov's descendants.This hugely influential aspect of his style did not come easily to him. He worried about endings. In 1889 he wrote, "My intuition tells me that it is in the conclusion of a story that I must manage ... to concentrate the impact that the whole of the story will leave on the reader and to do this, I must remind him, if only to a very small extent, of what has gone before." But he always questioned his work. He was never sure that his endings were right. In 1892 he said in a letter: "Those cursed denouements always escape me. The hero either has to get married or commit suicide – there seems to be no other alternative."

As he knew by then, there was another alternative, the Chekhov ending. He found it, and taught it by example to the writers of a whole century. Beneath it all there was a rule he followed consistently. Maintain the tension to the very last; never stop inserting precise detail, and then – just when the reader wonders how it can possibly end – stop.

PASSAGE JOUFFROY

Walter Benjamin, the Flâneur, and the Confetti of History

PASSAGE JOUFFROY, 'LES BOULEVARDS DE PARIS' (1877) A.-P MARTIAL. BIBLIOTHÈQUE NATIONALE DE FRANCE

Among those who love cities, who could fail to admire Walter Benjamin, that protean philosopher of urbanism, that poet of the sidewalk? In 1927 he began to study the workings of Paris from 1830 to 1870, when it was the capital of the nineteenth century and its entrepreneurs were inventing consumer capitalism. He focused on the shopping arcades, and to learn how they functioned he examined everything from newspaper advertising to Charles Baudelaire's poetry. In his own way, at once casual and brilliant, he made himself at home in that era and made it the subject of his great ambition.

As he saw it, the arcades, the ancestors of our shopping malls, existed as a city unto themselves, "a world in miniature" Physically, they were corridors with glass roofs and marble panelling, extending through entire blocks of buildings, where well-to-do Paris expressed its taste in the luxurious shops lining both sides of the corridors. Imaginatively they were much more. They were the generator of dreams, the place where society's ideas about excellence, charm, and style were formulated and spread. They were to their time what magazines like *Vogue*, *GQ*, and *Vanity Fair* are to ours.

Those carefully arranged spaces became "the theatre of all my struggles," Benjamin wrote. Here he would examine and judge even the most commonplace objects and ideas, revealing the true nature of their time and place. He dreamt of writing a new kind of history, liberating the past from the burden of standard narrative and instead presenting a crucial period through a careful collection of facts, ideas, images, minutiae, and esoterica. He wanted to add montage to the tools of the historian, "to assemble large-scale constructions out of the smallest and most precisely cut components. Indeed, to discover in the analysis of the small individual moment the crystal of the total event."

His friend Theodor Adorno, looking at the early drafts of the work he was doing, predicted in 1935 that the book would be one of the great philosophical achievements of the period. But in 1940, when Benjamin committed suicide in the Spanish Pyrenees because he feared he was about to fall into the hands of the Nazis, the project was far from complete. He had given years of his life to it, had filled thirty notebooks, but had never formulated the ideas that might have pulled it together.

Those ideas would naturally have been critical. Certainly they would have shown no friendliness toward the merchants and property developers who built the arcades. Benjamin was never a thorough-going Marxist, and certainly no great student of Marx's writings, but he was Marxist enough to distrust the very idea of organized retail business, secure in his belief (and the belief of most people he knew) that buying and selling could lead nowhere but to exploitation and imperialism. He was in certain ways the most accomplished German intellectual of his day, but he nevertheless suffered from the blindness that routinely afflicts intellectuals.

Exposing the dreams of the bourgeoisie, he never understood that he, too, was living in a dream, the Marxist dream of a society that, against all the odds, would be at once adventurous, free, honest, and egalitarian. He did his best to awaken humanity to the empty rapture of consumerism; but there was no one to awaken Benjamin.

Nor did he understand how shopping, and places where shops cluster, can help create a sense of community. The spirit of commerce, which animates so much of mankind, was alien to him. Today it's a commonplace that even the coldest and most forbidding institutions immediately become more approachable when a retail element is added. Consider, for instance, all the hospitals designed or renovated by Eberhard Zeidler, the Toronto architect, who has been heavily influenced by the ideas of the late Jane Jacobs. In his hands boring, empty spaces become busy, shared spaces through the introduction of retail atria. And shopping malls, in many ways the bastard children of the arcades (because franchised stores and relentless market research have made them so numbingly uniform), nevertheless function with some effect as secular gathering places in suburbs that have no other institutions playing that role.

For many years after his death, only a few scholars in Germany read the manuscript Benjamin had left behind. Tantalizingly, Adorno called it a significant document and other scholars quoted brief passages from it. In 1982 it finally appeared in Germany, and the 1,073-page English edition, *The Arcades Project*, translated by

Howard Eiland and Kevin McLaughlin, was published in 1999.

No one defended it as a book of theory. It's "a ruin filled with rid-dles," as one critic said. Examining it, we feel like scholars studying the research notes for a masterpiece that was never written. It lacks, to put it mildly, shapeliness. It points in all directions and none; it raises issues that never get developed, and it betrays on every page the failure of the author's good intentions. It's like a city from antiquity that exists as rubble, rumour, and mystery, a Pompeii of scholarship.

The first-class reporter accumulates facts until, properly sort-ed, they turn into knowledge; in the hands of a fact-gatherer like Benjamin, the process moves to another level, toward illumination. Benjamin knew that God is in the details – and so is everything else, including the understanding of society. There was always a religious aspect to his work. As Peter Brier wrote in an essay called "Walter Benjamin's sparks of holiness" for the *Southwest Review* : "He was at once the Talmudist laboriously testing each of the forty-nine inter-pretations, the Kabbalist searching for sparks of holiness embedded in the encrusted debris of the past, and the Marxist pursuing his dialectical path."

Assembling his material, Benjamin created sections carrying titles like "Dream City," "Boredom," "the Seine," and "Fashion." He noted the Parisian craze for cashmere shawls and chronicled the promise of Marquis Chocolates (44 Rue Vivienne, at the Passage des Panoramas), which in 1846 announced that a selection of verses ("from the year's purest, most gracious, and most elevated publications") would be included in the package with its exquisite confections.

Benjamin wrote about art galleries, prostitution, streetcars, illu-minated gardens, and every other subject his eye fell on. He reported his discovery that in 1867 the velvet-bound menu at Les Trois Frères Provençaux ran for 36 pages and offered, among other things, 71 varieties of compote.

No one had ever before taken such pains to gather up the confetti of modern history. He worked like an archeologist uncovering a corner of the Roman Empire, studying his fragments of stone in the hope they would eventually make sense. Till Benjamin, no theorist had thought to borrow the Balzacian and Dickensian technique of bringing an era to life through attention to its most minute cultural details. Since Benjamin, however, thousands of essayists, critics, and professors of cultural studies have taken the same course, not always to good effect. Students in cultural studies, apparently reasoning that they are entitled to do whatever they think Benjamin did, have a habit of producing essays that contain almost nothing but quotations. They miss the point that Benjamin went deep into the archives for obscure detail; students sometimes think that one quotation is as good as another and even quote Benjamin himself.

On a more serious level, the most distinguished descendants of Benjamin include Susan Sontag, when she shuffled through science fiction to find the spirit of her times, Roland Barthes, who wrote about Garbo's face, and Marshall McLuhan when he pondered the implications of advertising and Dagwood Bumstead.

Graduate students have been stimulated to write uncounted theses about *The Arcades Project*, but otherwise it sits on the shelf, accumulating (as Woody Allen once said of his old copies of the *New York Review*) thick layers of dust and guilt. Reading *The Arcades Project* is impossible. It can be consulted; it can be paged through; it can be looked into; but no one (aside from translators, editors, and reviewers) has ever claimed to have read it straight through, as one reads someone like Barthes.

If we judge it as a persuasive account of its subject, then it will always be considered a failure. On the other hand, it's a magnificent failure, an endlessly interesting and surprising failure, a failure that only a great and ingenious writer could leave us. Or, as Frank Kermode wrote, there are more systematic minds, but there are few that match Benjamin's intuitive power – "the informing eye, the inquiring spirit." All the articles written since *The Arcades Project* appeared have only added to Benjamin's stature, though no one has so far tried to emulate the grandeur of his vision.

When Benjamin and the arcades are mentioned, the flâneur inevitably elbows his way into the conversation. This is the sprightliest and most suggestive element in Benjamin's book, the portrait of a particular male type who moved comfortably through the arcades and helped create their character. He crops up often in *The Arcades Project*, as apparently he once did in Paris, but he also gets a special section of his own in the book, 39 pages long.

Benjamin saw in him an emblem of Parisian life. The flâneur, he believed, expressed the political attitude of the middle classes during the Second Empire – withdrawn, uncommitted, observant but not deeply involved, proud but not noticeably articulate, sometimes sinister. For all that, Benjamin could not dislike him. He enjoyed the fellow's style and shared his pleasure in the discoveries of curious phenomena.

North American civilization has never made a place for the flâneur. As the late Anatole Broyard of the *New York Times* once noted, "Our boulevards, such as they are, are not avenues for the parade and observation of personality, or for perusal by the flâneur, but conveyor belts to the stores, where we can buy everything but human understanding."

Even defining the word has never been easy for North Americans. A French-English dictionary will tell you it means "a stroller," nothing more. But on this subject the usually mild-mannered *American Heritage Dictionary* suddenly reveals intense hostility. A flâneur, it says, is "an aimless idler; a loafer." Webster calls him "an idle man-about-town," though a true flâneur would insist that there's nothing idle about the search for sensation, gossip, and unexpected human beauty.

In studying the flâneur Benjamin followed Baudelaire, the writer who obsessed him more than any other. In Baudelaire we meet the flâneur as a supercilious dandy, alienated from the crowd through which he walks, an aristocrat in his own eyes if not in anyone else's. He dresses well, though he's not necessarily prosperous; at one point Benjamin depicts him returning alone to a single room. As we follow Benjamin on his stroll through the arcades, Benjamin follows the flâneur.

A flâneur never hurries; Baudelaire says that in Paris there was a brief vogue for walking turtles on a leash, so that one's turtle could set the proper pace for a flânerie. So far as I know, the flâneur has made only one notable appearance, en masse, in Canadian history.

That was on the site of Expo 67 in Montreal. Expo, in fact, could have been designed with the needs of the flâneur in mind. The architecture was often amazing; the paths connecting the buildings emphasized surprise; there were no cars to disturb the contemplative mood of the stroller, and the on-site population always included a remarkable number of beautiful females (by good fortune, that was the year the miniskirt reached its apogee). I spent four months there, and even I walked slowly, taking it all in. I noticed a good many men who might well be classified as flâneurs, though I saw no one with a turtle.

For years I have aspired to the status of at least a part-time flâneur, but something has always kept it beyond my reach. I blame the presence within me of the pale vestiges of Protestantism, a gentle but oppressively persistent fog which clouded the world around me during my Toronto childhood. We learn most when we least know we are learning; I believe I learned, without knowing it, that there was no place in our world for someone whose main joy was observation and whose main interest was noting, often with a certain disdain, the varieties of humans in his path. I walk, but usually with a purpose. I wander, but not for long; soon I look for a bench where I can read.

The flâneur exalts purposelessness – which is, literally, against my religion and my community's religion. Sad to say, my experience of serious flânerie remains mainly literary and no doubt always will. Happily, however, Walter Benjamin's awkward masterwork provides the would-be flâneur with a wonderfully capacious boulevard for the imagination.

The Life and Times
of the *Partisan Review*

I

n the middle of the twentieth century the leading American intellectual magazine rarely sold more than 10,000 copies but nevertheless had a greater effect on opinion and the course of literature than publications many times its size. The triumph of the *Partisan Review* was something no one could have predicted, given that the magazine's origins were narrowly ideological and its point of view was passionate yet never entirely coherent.

The *Partisan Review* began life in 1934 within the John Reed Club, a subsidiary of the Communist Party and therefore one of the many overseas extensions of Stalinism. The young editors, William Phillips and Philip Rahv, were Marxists with a literary bent. They soon found that their backers expected them to favour Soviet ideology at the expense of literary standards and the independence of their writers.

After nine difficult issues they broke away from the club and from the Communist Party. This was no small gesture in the Greenwich Village leftist circles of the time. Phillips and Rahv were branded as traitors to the cause and "slanderers of the working class." Certain close friends, loyal Communists, immediately became sworn enemies.

They suspended publication for fourteen months, then re-appeared with new writers and a slowly evolving editorial view. With the infamous show trials in Moscow and then the Nazi-Soviet alliance, they grew into vehement critics of Stalin, perhaps his most articulate and thoughtful American enemies.

That change was the first of many. PR never became entirely political, but it remained permanently leftist, to some degree or another, even after certain contributors, notably Norman Podhoretz, moved over to neo-conservatism. But its precise status on the continuum of socialism was never easy to describe.

While editors and contributors were deeply interested in politics, it was not the kind identified with Democrats, Republicans, or even American socialists. It was a highly theorized and romantic version, an imported politics, an approach to public life grounded in Marxist analysis. For a time their views reflected those of Leon Trotsky and his followers, who believed they could somehow

EDITORIAL STAFF OF PARTISAN REVIEW. FROM LEFT: FRED DUPEE, GEORGE MORRIS, PHILIP RAHV, WILLIAM PHILLIPS, DWIGHT MACDONALD. PHOTO: MAURY GARBER put the Russian revolution (and the many revolutions that would inevitably follow) back on the true course. But at the same time (and unlike almost every other Marxist magazine on the planet), PR saw itself as a defender and explicator of avant-garde culture.

These two spheres of interest, dealt with separately by most of journalism, were allowed to mingle and affect each other in the pages of PR. To both of them PR brought intellectual toughness and sharply focused polemical energy. That quality proved especially influential. Many an essayist, in North America and Europe, took heart from the ability of PR writers to shake off the charms of easygoing prose and instead state their arguments with forthright vigour. As a reader of PR from 1953, I realized that it was infecting my own style, always (in my view) for the better. It was also opening me to an astonishing array of exotic ideas.

The editors favoured writers on politics who also had literary credentials. Over the years they provided an American outlet for Camus, Koestler, Sartre, and other Europeans. George Orwell was a close reader of PR and a valuable contributor; beginning in 1941, he wrote the magazine's "London Letter" on fifteen occasions.

At the same time, articles on avant-garde literature, painting, and music showed the effects of Marxism. Clement Greenberg, the art critic, brought to the world of museums and galleries the supreme confidence of the Marxist intellectual, along with the frequently accusatory tone that Marxism encouraged.

He was the first of the PR writers whose influence was felt far beyond the magazine and even beyond the US. Almost alone among critics, he gave Abstract Expressionism thorough, serious attention and recognized its international significance. In the March 1948 issue he broke the stunning news that the new American painters, including Jackson Pollock and Willem de Kooning, were world leaders:

> When one sees how much the level of American art has risen in the last five years, the conclusion forces itself, much of our own surprise, that the main premises of Western art have at last migrated to the United States, along with the center of gravity of industrial production and political power.

Many an art critic, in America and elsewhere, found that statement outrageously chauvinistic. But in the years that followed, no one successfully refuted it. Greenberg, though he wrote seldom, became the most influential art critic since Ruskin, constantly quoted, as often reviled as praised.

From the beginning PR was the outlet of a mainly Jewish circle that became known as the New York Intellectuals. They were Jews in background and personal culture, many of them the children of East European immigrants who were educated at City College, but they showed little interest in Jewish affiliation, either in synagogues or in Zionism. In their collective imagination they were universalists, like good Marxists; they saw no virtue in parochial causes. Nor were they (in the pages of PR) particularly concerned about antisemitism. They treated T.S. Eliot as a critic of towering stature, though no one was ignorant of his negative view of Jews. Ezra Pound and his role in modern poetry were always taken seriously, long after his affections for fascism were demonstrated.

Philip Rahv produced literary criticism, and Edmund Wilson contributed to PR. But among literary critics the grand figure was Lionel Trilling, whose grave, majestic prose, delicately echoing Matthew Arnold, gave a certain grandeur to every issue in which he appeared. A reader could sense that he was trying to tell us that something crucial was at stake, something that deeply mattered, in every book he discussed. Moral seriousness was the core of his subject, the mission of his life. Today his literary passion has mainly vanished from the American intellectual conversation, but one can still feel its effects in the work of the great American writer, Phillip Roth.

Saul Bellow's early career was, arguably, a product of PR. The editors singled him out for attention, writing about him and publishing his work. And for a 1953 issue Bellow translated from the Yiddish a short story by Isaac Bashevis Singer, "Gimpel the Fool." That piece created widespread interest in Singer's work and led to his international career as the most widely translated Yiddish writer in history. It also turned out to be a historic coup for PR, a collaboration of two men who would each win the Nobel Prize two decades later, an ambitious literary editor's ultimate dream.

The magazine lasted till 2003, but the serious decline of its influence began in the mid-1960s. Perhaps predictably, given the pattern of internecine warfare, *PR* was destroyed from within, by words printed on its own pages. But the fatal blow was the result of neither the familiar hubris of star writers nor the constant dispute between the two main editors, Phillips and Rahv, whose mutual dislike and disdain were by then the subject of derisive or worried gossip.

The blow was delivered by an outsider, Susan Sontag, a 31-year-old who had read the *PR* writers since early adolescence. She believed above all in the heritage of high culture for which they stood, and yet wrote in all innocence the famous article that did more than anything else to unravel the magazine's ideals. No one understood it at the time, but from the perspective of a later century it seems clear that Sontag's first and most famous article, "Notes On 'Camp,'" published first by *PR* in 1964 and then in her book of essays *Against Interpretation*, weakened the magazine's tone, trivialized its ideas, and undermined its unique stature within American culture.

Submitting it to *PR* was a stroke of public relations genius for Sontag. In another journal it would have been amusing and in certain ways stimulating. In the normally solemn pages of *PR* it read more like a manifesto. Perhaps it was a parody of a manifesto (with numbered paragraphs like a political argument and eccentric, aggressively phrased conclusions). It raised a troublesome question: was it a parody of the idea of Camp, until then recognized as a mainly homosexual taste? Or did it parody *PR* itself?

Sontag explained that the essence of Camp, a private code and a badge of identity, lies in its love of artifice and exaggeration. She defined Camp as a sensibility that converts the serious into the frivolous. She named Camp specifics from Tiffany lamps to Flash Gordon comics, from 1920s couture (feather boas, beaded dresses) to Art Nouveau and Gaudí's "lurid and beautiful buildings" in Barcelona.

Sexuality plays a large role in her essay:

> *Camp taste draws on a mostly unacknowledged truth of taste:*
> *the most refined form of sexual attractiveness (as well as the most*
> *refined form of sexual pleasure) consists in going against the grain*

of one's sex. What is most beautiful in virile men is something feminine; what is most beautiful in feminine women is something masculine.

She cited the flamboyance of actresses such as Jayne Mansfield, Gina Lollobrigida, and Jane Russell and the he-man qualities of Steve Reeves and Victor Mature. She set Camp taste against the seriousness of high culture. "The whole point of Camp is to dethrone the serious." She championed Camp taste as a mode of enjoyment and appreciation rather than judgment. "It relishes, rather than judges." It incarnates, she announced, a victory of style over content, aesthetics over morality, and irony over tragedy.

But surely PR had told us, in a dozen different ways, that "the tragic sense of life" is an essential part of everyone's intellectual equipment. Furthermore, judging by the most severe standards was one of the magazine's central functions. And of course moral seriousness was its chosen attitude, ideology, and tone of voice.

Sontag's article made her the anti-Trilling, the anti-Greenberg. Her words were quoted in *Time* magazine and eventually in half the magazines and newspapers across the world. She arrived at the perfect moment, just as Pop Art (which Greenberg despised) was establishing itself. Sontag and Pop Art reinforced each other's message of unjudged, innocent, playful culture. Marshall McLuhan's view that advertising art contained some of the most powerful cultural influences of modern times was confirmed. Serious essays on the Beatles and comic books followed. In the arts a new era was born. PR, despite some frantic attempts to catch up, had no place in the cultural world that was unfolding.

In the early days PR writers and readers shook with rage at the effect of Stalinism on culture, above all American culture. In 1946 the editors accused the two most important liberal magazines, the *New Republic* and the *Nation*, of "licking Stalin's boots." Stalin's death in 1953, and the declining prestige of the USSR among American liberals, robbed PR of its favourite enemy.

One odd result, apparently, was to intensify the increasingly bitter struggle between Phillips and Rahv, whose relationship was sometimes described as a marriage that survived only for the sake of *PR*, their child.

By common agreement Phillips was the harder worker. He constantly worried about getting the magazine published (funding was always a problem) and striking the proper balance of subject matter and opinion. Also by common agreement, Rahv was the more brilliant editor; on his best days he could get first-class prose from writers who would become stars of American letters. As a critic he published rarely but always impressively. Rahv's renowned ego, and his habit of rating his importance in literature even higher than that of his contributors, was a frequent subject of conversation around the magazine, often introduced by Phillips. He diagnosed Rahv as a "manic-impressive" but claimed that psychoanalysis would do him no good: "Most of us, under analysis, break down and admit our shortcomings." But, he conjectured, Rahv "would break down and confess he was a great man."

In 1965 the board nominally in charge of the magazine decided to end three decades of bickering by naming Phillips the editor. Rahv, enraged, sued for control. It mystified lawyers acting for both sides: how could a company that had no assets, had never made a profit and never expected to, be the subject of litigation? Phillips recalled the case as a bizarre comedy, concocted by Rahv out of perverse amusement: "Only an intransigent revolutionary mind, deeply immersed in the tradition of Marxism, could have thought up such a parody of capitalist property relations." Rahv had to settle for a minor role in *PR* and in 1969 went off to start his own short-lived magazine, *Modern Occasions*. Two universities, first Rutgers and then Boston University, published *PR* for the rest of its life.

Phillips died in 2002, and the magazine closed down the following year. When I heard about its demise I looked up an essay Leslie A. Fiedler had written about the magazine in 1956 for *Perspectives*, a short-lived journal published by the Ford Foundation. A brilliant contributor in the 1940s and 1950s, Fiedler said he, like many *PR* writers, "wanted desperately to feel that the struggle for revolutionary politics and the highest literary standards was a single struggle" but, as the years passed, had trouble continuing to believe in this PR principle.

Fiedler quoted an unnamed contributor (the context suggests it was Saul Bellow) who said of PR that "I never took that dodo for a Phoenix." Fiedler said it was not a publication anyone loved; only its enemies were passionate. Actually, some readers, like me, did love it. And for all its pretensions it was in its time close to a convincing literary parallel of the richly plumed mythical firebird and symbol of culture that the Persians and Greeks called a Phoenix; as close, in fact, as any English-language literary journal published in the twentieth century.

H.G. Wells and
the Wages of Adultery

H.G. WELLS, 1920S. LIBRARY OF CONGRESS

T he delicate and evocative word "passade" sprays a mist of
romance over what our blunter era calls a fling, a one-night
stand, a hook-up or, more often, an affair. "Passade" derives
from a fifteenth-century French term meaning "portion of a game."
At various times the same word has described a certain move in
fencing, an exercise in horsemanship, and a gift of alms to a stranger. The fourth meaning cited in the OED, the one that appears here
and there in literature, is "a brief romance." You can find it in Byron,
Edith Wharton, and P. G. Wodehouse. It was a key word in the vocabulary of H.G. Wells, a prolific and grandly successful author in the
first half of the twentieth century, also renowned (in a somewhat less
public way) for his ambitious and spectacularly extensive sex life.

Wells had sexual relationships with about 100 women (coinciden-
tally, he wrote roughly the same number of books), and he began
each affair in the hope of enjoying a passade – a liaison that would be
controlled and controllable, ending in happiness all around.

To his dismay, however, the results were often the opposite of
what he intended. The most famous case was his tempestuous and
at times bitter relationship with Rebecca West, also a writer of great
distinction. Over their ten years as lovers she was often disappointed
and often angry; he was more or less permanently apologetic. She
expected him to abandon his convenient but mostly sexless marriage
to marry her – except on those frequent occasions when she insisted,
to the contrary, that she wanted only to remain single and independent. By inadvertence they had a son, Anthony West, also a writer,
born in 1914, whose furious and increasingly public struggle against
his mother lasted for most of the twentieth century and did not end
until they both died, she in 1983, he in 1987. Together H.G., Rebecca,
and Anthony created a legend in which love and ambition mingled
with literature, betrayal, and profound rage.

The carefully justified romantic life of Wells provides both the
theme and the narrative energy of an impressive book, David Lodge's
A Man of Parts (2011), a 565-page biographical novel. Lodge absorbed
a library of letters and diaries and then unleashed his imagination
on the private details, fitting his fictional dialogue and events within
the known facts.

ROBERT FULFORD

He has much to tell us about Wells the prophet, who dreamt of
world government, put his faith in human reason and foresaw the
internet, aerial warfare, nuclear bombs, and television, among much
else. This was the Wells who tried to encompass all that is known
about the human past with his 1,324-page *The Outline of History*, a
work of unparalleled clunkiness, unreadable now but a worldwide
smash in 1920. Lodge also chronicles Wells the science-fiction
novelist, who inspired generations of writers and filmmakers with
The *Time Machine* (1895) and *The War of the Worlds* (1898), and Wells
the domestic novelist, who loved making fiction from his own story
of a wretchedly poor lad who rises to eminence by nerve, energy,
and good luck; his favourite version, and the public's, was *Kipps: The
Story of a Simple Soul* (1905). Nor does Lodge ignore the hard political
work that Wells put in at the Fabian Society as it created a theoretical
base for democratic socialism. Wells even tried to dominate the Fabians, in the name of modernization, before being thwarted by, among
others, his sometimes friend George Bernard Shaw.

But those versions of Wells pale, in Lodge's telling, beside Wells
the relentless and always optimistic seducer. "As I gradually got
deeper into Wells' network of relationships," Lodge said, "I began
to get some idea of his extraordinary sexual life and the trouble it
caused him. He never seemed to learn from it, getting himself into
more and more hot water."

Today it's impossible to read of Wells and sexuality without comparing his time and ours. Today a public figure caught in adultery is
universally condemned as a lying scoundrel who must be punished. If
the law cannot deal with him then the media will see that he's properly shamed. Former senator John Edwards or former governor Arnold
Schwarzenegger, former Prime Minister Silvio Berlusconi, or golfer
Tiger Woods – in television, newspaper, and internet discussions they
are all convicted of callously breaking their marriage vows.

They are fair game for every anchor person or family therapist who
cares to pass judgment, as many do. If anyone in this position hopes
to recover the love of the public he must at minimum apologize in
public for the harm he has done to his wife and all those who love
him. "I am deeply ashamed of my terrible judgment" are the words

uttered by an American congressman caught messaging close-up
photos of his crotch on Facebook. That's the required tone. He may
explain himself by claiming that he suffers from sex addiction or
some other medically approved condition. What he will not do is
defend himself by justifying adultery.

But Wells, far from making a general apology for adultery, elevated
it to the level of a social theory. What he liked was recreational lovemaking, harmless fun, but nothing so simple could satisfy a man of
the future. He was a feminist, like all Fabians, and women had to be
included in the theory. He invented something he called "triangular
mutuality," a practice on which a man, wife, and mistress would
agree. No one would object, and all would be expressing their free
choice. As Orwell wrote, responding to some outlandish political
schemer, no ordinary man in the street could come up with such an
idea; only an intellectual could be that stupid.

The record shows in Wells' case that neither of his two wives nor
any of his other inamoratas showed any enthusiasm for this arrange-
ment; the best response he could elicit from them was a grudging
silence. Nevertheless he liked the phrase and persisted in using it.

Wells' desire for a quiet passade often got him into hideous trouble. At one point he and an extremely young woman agreed to consummate their relationship on a trip to Paris but were intercepted by
her apoplectic father at Paddington Station just after boarding the
boat train. Another lover, unwilling to be dismissed by Wells, needed
emergency medical attention after she showed up at his house and
slit her wrists in his presence. A third woman, pregnant by Wells,
had to be persuaded to marry her second choice, an agreeable but
unexciting young man who generously accepted her situation.

Wells considered himself, in matters of sexuality, a creative thinker, potentially a benefactor of humanity. In his view he was freeing
everyone. Were these the arguments of a charlatan? Was Wells, to
use another old-fashioned term, a complete humbug? When it was
all over he seems to have acknowledged a certain regret. In 1934, aged
68, he wrote his *Experiment in Autobiography*. He discussed his love
affairs in a separate postscript and directed that this section not be
published until half a century had passed. As he said himself, "My

story of my relations with women is mainly a story of greed, foolishness and great expectation."

In 1913, when Rebecca West met Wells, she was a prodigiously talented 21-year-old literary critic. From the beginning she had a way of combining details from everyday life in generalizations about culture and morality. An early review included a line frequently quoted since: "The power to create a work of art, like a good complexion, is frequently bestowed on the undeserving."

Her negative review of a Wells novel, *Marriage*, so intrigued him that he invited her to lunch. Soon they were lovers. In bed she called him "Jaguar," and he called her "Panther." The intensity of their lovemaking was matched by the ferocity of their arguments. Wells could be irascible, but West was capable of monumental anger. She was easily hurt and managed to be hurt many times by almost everyone she knew. A London journalist, Charles Curran, diagnosed her as a case of "psychological haemophilia." She bled profusely at the slightest prick of criticism. "Like many people so afflicted, she was wholly unaware that others could also bleed."

That same hyper-sensitivity enlivened her prose, both in her novels and her non-fiction. Her material was set forth with a combination of total clarity and impassioned immediacy. She made a reputation as one of the most readable serious writers in English; as a stylist she was easily superior to Wells.

Her 1941 book on the history and culture of Yugoslavia, *Black Lamb and Grey Falcon*, has had devoted readers for over 75 years, and her reporting for the *New Yorker*, collected in books like *A Train of Powder* (1955) and *The Meaning of Treason* (1947), established her as one of the best journalists of the postwar years. She was beautiful as well as richly accomplished, a desirable woman who had affairs with Lord Beaverbrook and the American journalist John Gunther, among others. To the end of her days she was a celebrity; in 1981 Warren Beatty gave her a brief part in his film *Reds*. But, as all her friends knew and the world would soon find out, her life was grievously marred (in her own view) by her struggle with her son.

In the early 1950s I often read with intense enjoyment Anthony West's literary essays in the *New Yorker*. As a would-be critic, I saw them as one kind of model. In dealing with literary history he expressed a sharply focused passion that gave his articles (in my young eyes) a sense that something crucial was at stake. I remember particularly his anger when describing the unconscionable way Oscar Wilde's defenceless children were treated after his death. West handled a subject like that without any sense of critical distance; the reader was expected to share his indignation. What I didn't understand was that an unappeasable self-pity lay behind his work, the result of his belief that his life had been blighted by an outrageously unfair childhood.

Early in the twentieth century there was no established social protocol for "single mother." As a boy Anthony lived with Rebecca, but she had no idea how to talk to him about their situation. Sometimes she asked that he treat her as his aunt when others were around. Wells came to visit them but never for long; he was to be called "Wellsie," not "Father." Some friends and servants knew the truth; others didn't know or were asked to hide their knowledge. Anthony found himself conscripted to play a role in a drama where the script was always changing. He was made to feel that he was an inconvenience to his mother, and he resented the frequent absences her working life required. In later years she claimed that she had always been a good mother, but one of her biographers remarked: "Rebecca eventually admitted that sending Anthony away to school at the age of three was a mistake." When he turned out to be a less than admirable student she did not hide her dissatisfaction.

Rebecca's sister, Lettie, suggested to Wells at one point that Anthony found the question of his parentage disturbing. Perhaps it should be carefully explained. Wells replied that he knew about boys and knew that "a boy had no natural desire to know about his parents." That was a silly bourgeois notion. Lettie wondered "whether H.G. was the cleverest man in England or a silly little fool."

Anthony continued to burn with indignation, and in 1955, when he was in his forties, he shared his feelings with the world. His novel *Heritage* was about a boy named Richard Savage, after the eighteenth-century poet who claimed he was a bastard abandoned by his cruel mother. The story had its comic side, but it was principally the tragic tale of a child neglected by famous parents.

888

Young Richard's father came out of it better than his mother, which reflected Anthony's views. He always loved Wells, re-enacting a familiar pattern by favouring the parent who didn't have to do the day-to-day rearing. Moreover, when Wells managed to be present he must have seemed the more attentive parent. He had the successful seducer's gift of focusing on one individual as if no one else in the world mattered.

Rebecca West let it be known that if *Heritage* were published in Britain she would sue the publishers for libel. It didn't appear in England till 1984, the year after her death.

That same year Anthony West had another of his books published in England, *H.G. Wells: Aspects of a Life*, which he called "a memoir-biography." He had worked on it for many years, and it was to be his last book, an affectionate, admiring portrait of Wells – and one final attack on Rebecca. *The New York Times* reviewer called it an enthralling biography, marred mainly by the fact that West kept coming "back to the subject of Rebecca West, who, when all is written, is the ultimate target of his book." This was surely the ultimate case of a passade that did not turn out as H.G. Wells hoped.

The Inscrutable Mystery of Faces

FRANZ JOSEPH GALL LEADING A DISCUSSION ON PHRENOLOGY, THOMAS ROWLANDSON, 1808

I f you poke carefully at our language, it reveals the past in all its squalor, its ignorance, and its poignant dreams of enlightenment. For instance, when an intellectual of today writes a book such as Lawrence W. Levine's *Highbrow/Lowbrow: The Emergence of Cultural Hierarchy in America* (1988), why does he find it convenient to use words referring to facial characteristics? Why do any of us speak of comic books as "lowbrow," Proust as "highbrow"? What in the world is the relationship between a brow and intelligence or taste? Why did I, in youth, learn to dismiss sentimental movies and books as "middlebrow," a term of contempt?

Pry those words open, and a wondrously odd passage in cultural history falls out. The answers go back many hundreds of years and take us into the realm of folk culture, the beliefs that everyone knows are true until, in some cases, we learn they aren't. The earth is flat, as any fool can plainly see, and the sun goes around the earth. Who would ever guess otherwise? Not me. In the same way, people have believed for centuries that we can assess the character and intelligence of our fellow human beings by examining their faces. Many still believe it, and (I argue) there are those who maintain that belief unconsciously while thinking that they have rejected it. I have caught myself saying of someone, "Of course he's a con man. He almost has CON MAN stencilled on his forehead." Then I catch myself; in truth, before I knew what he did, and what he said, I would have had no way of knowing whether he was one of nature's liars. His face – admit it! – told me nothing by itself. Many years ago I came to know slightly a bearded man who looked to me exactly like the imaginary portraits of biblical prophets I'd studied in a few dozen museums. To this museumgoer his face spoke of probity, intelligence, vision, perhaps even poetry. Then I came to know him a little and discovered he was mean, paranoid, quick to anger, and given to jealousy, a rather ugly fellow to know.

The study of faces amounts to a study of the shaky relationship between evidence and intuition. The Greeks believed they could read faces, and produced poetry on that theme. Aristotle wrote "we shall be able to infer character from features," and no one saw any reason to disagree with him. In fact, we should all be experts in reading faces; we spend much of our lives looking into the faces of friends, relatives, and lovers. It seems to follow that this experience gives us the ability to know by mere observation that one man is evil and another one is not, that this woman speaks the truth and that one doesn't. If we try in vain to understand the face of a familiar friend or enemy we will almost certainly come to think that an answer lies somewhere – just as many believe God made the world because other possibilities seem even more unlikely. We have infinite confidence in knowledge that should exist but for which there's no proof. Something makes us believe that for every puzzle we will eventually find an answer.

When Western science arrived among us a few centuries ago it naturally continued to explore what could be learned from faces. Thomas Browne (1605-1682), the great physician-philosopher, tried to hoist what we might call "face wisdom" up onto one of the lower plateaus of theology. In his first book, *Religio Medici* (1643), he used the term "physiognomy," which is nowadays defined as "The supposed art of judging character from facial characteristics" the operative word being "supposed." There was no "supposed" in Browne's thinking. He argued that there were certain inspired people who (even if they were unable to read books) could look into faces and see the content of souls. In a later book, *Christian Morals*, he elaborated on that point: "Since the Brow speaks often true, since Eyes and Noses have Tongues, and the countenance proclaims the heart and inclinations," anyone can see the "Physiognomical" truth. He went farther: "there are therefore Provincial Faces, National Lips and Noses."

Still, those ideas were often dismissed as fraudulent in the Middle Ages, and in the Renaissance they were still in bad odour. Physiognomy sometimes claimed to predict the future: this is what will happen to a man with this face. So Henry VIII outlawed it, as he outlawed palm-reading; they were both the occupations of the criminal class. Leonardo was a sceptic about the claims of physiognomy: "There is no truth in them and this can be proven because these chimeras have no scientific foundation." All this was speculation, of course. But in another century or two eager researchers began trying to turn physiognomy into a legitimate science.

Johann Kaspar Lavater (1741-1801), a Swiss pastor and a friend of Goethe, breathed new life into the subject. He studied Browne, along with other earlier sages, and believed he recognized the truth. Lavater's essays were accompanied by illustrations with heavy-handed captions: "A Face disfigured by Idleness and Debauchery" or "Heads expressing Inhuman Satisfaction, from Voltaire's self-sufficient Sneer, up to an Infernal Grin." Lavater was a true believer: "With secret ecstasy the benevolent Physiognomist penetrates into the interior of his fellow-creature. Thus he judges Man only by himself."

Lavater's books sold across Europe and provoked discussion. Writers were attracted to physiognomic thinking; it influenced the descriptions of characters in Balzac, Dickens, Hardy, and Charlotte Brontë. Oscar Wilde made physiognomy an underlying assumption of *The Picture of Dorian Gray* (1890) and justified the premise with an often-quoted line: "It is only shallow people who do not judge by appearances. The true mystery of the world is the visible, not the invisible."

Would-be scientists competed to develop proven systems of face wisdom. They enormously expanded what we could see (or believed we could see) by looking at a face. Researchers would measure the faces of criminals and claim they had discovered a fair, objective way to judge the accused in criminal courts. But the statistical evidence gathered in this way tended to be more hopeful than credible. A good many researchers developed the habit of discarding facts that led nowhere and reporting only those that buttressed their theories.

Nevertheless, these widely publicized findings affected conversation, journalism, and literature. The phrase "chinless wonder" became a widespread insult, as applied to young men in Britain who had acquired good positions through nepotism; their recessive chins were assumed to be the result of inbreeding among the upper classes. A man with a chiselled, sculpted mouth, it was reckoned, would turn out to be strong and perhaps dangerous. A small face, with eyes close to each other, suggests a poor character. An aquiline nose (also called a Roman nose or a hook nose), which appears to be curved or bent, indicates vision and intelligence, possibly heroism; aquiline comes from the Latin for "eagle-like."

All this, and much more, the advocates of physiognomy spread around the world. All were rejected in the end, and their occupation has since been routinely classified as a pseudo-science. But it is not dead yet. In recent years the *Economist*, *Slate*, and the *New Statesman* have all carried sceptical but still respectful reports of experiments that seem to suggest that there might, just possibly, be something that can be rescued from the historic collapse of physiognomy. So far the results are only marginally interesting, but physiognomy has left behind a residue that some scientists find worth exploring. It has also left us the brow question, mentioned above. Dr Franz Joseph Gall (1758-1828), a German doctor, founded craniology, a would-be science later called phrenology. An appropriately trained person could put his hands on someone's skull, grope around a bit, then judge the subject's intelligence, character, etc. Gall believed that people with large foreheads have bigger brains. (Portraits show that Gall himself had a generous-sized brow.)

As a result, in 1875 "highbrow" became a synonym for intellectual. In 1902 this led naturally to a new word, "lowbrow" In 1949 this curious terminology grew more popular. Russell Lynes wrote a witty article in *Harper's*, entitled "Highbrow, Lowbrow, Middlebrow," and *Life* magazine made it famous by running a chart illustrating in cartoons the tastes of the different brow levels in America as Lynes described them. In an accompanying article Winthrop Sargeant, a music critic, declared himself proudly highbrow; one of his highbrow characteristics, he said, was his refusal to smoke any pipe tobacco that stooped to advertising. Those articles inaugurated a parlour game in which readers rated their own brow levels and those of their friends.

There was another contribution to brow theory. Studies of Neanderthals showed they had short necks, ridges on their brows, and sloping foreheads. They were, to be sure, lowbrows. But so, on the other hand, were many prominent modern humans. Winston Churchill and Steve Jobs had similar sloping foreheads, brow ridges, etc.

Whatever the reason, writers came to love the noble brow. They made brows into a characteristic element in literature. For decades books, good and bad, teemed with men and women whose brows were called admirable. Robert Burns, gazing at a portrait of an earl, praised "that noble, dauntless brow." H. Rider Haggard, in *She* (1886), admired a woman's "great changing eyes of deepest, softest black, of the tinted face, of the broad and noble brow." Harriet Beecher Stowe, in *Uncle Tom's Cabin* (1852) , grew rapturous over a "fair, high-bred child, with her golden head, her deep eyes, her spiritual, noble brow." L.M. Montgomery in *The Blue Castle* (1926) hymned a "noble brow, a straight, classic nose, lips and chin and cheek modelled as if some goddess of old time had sat to the sculptor." This literary cliché has followed us even into the twenty-first century. John Banville in *Eclipse* (2000) has a character refer to "My brand-new father-in-law, a watchful widower with the incongruously noble brow of a philosopher king."

A strange closing chapter of this story was written in Mumbai in 2008. Among the Pakistani killers who conducted a sudden terrorist attack on the city, killing as many people as they could, only one was captured alive, Ajmal Kasab. He was as vicious a killer as the world has known. He had no particular interest in religion or politics but joined the terrorist team because they fed him and paid him a salary. As soon as the Mumbai police gave him food he went over to their side and provided the details of the atrocity. That didn't save him from being hanged, but it left us an interesting anecdote about what we can or can't learn by studying faces.

He was a nice-looking fellow, when he wasn't being dragged around by the police. He was 20 years old, five feet tall, and possessed of an innocent round face. He had bright eyes and apple cheeks. The newspapers called him "the baby-faced killer." A columnist in the *Times of India* asked: "Who or what is he? Dangerous fanatic or exploited innocent?" Aside from being a monster, he was another proof that faces tell us exactly nothing about the character of individual humans.

Sigmund Freud and the Daimon of Literature

Lionel Trilling, a great literary critic, dreamt of becoming an equally eminent writer of fiction. In middle age, however, he admitted to his journal that he lacked two necessary qualities. He defined them in Yiddish terms – "chutzpah" (nerve) and "meshugas" (craziness), attributes that he envied when he noted their appearance in such famous contemporaries as Norman Mailer and Saul Bellow. Trilling, mired in a straitlaced corner of academe, needed an explosive charge to crack open his secret self.

Sigmund Freud, whom Trilling studied and wrote about, began with a similar problem but solved it – or, rather, had it solved by accident. As Freud acknowledged, he acquired a "daimon," a wild force, a creature who (like the daimons inhabiting ancient literature) inspired him to dare, to step boldly outside prescribed thinking, and to admit that he possessed certain impulses that no truly respectable nineteenth-century citizen of Vienna should for a moment entertain. Freud's daimon helped give him the courage of his own originality.

By tradition daimons appear in unexpected forms, and that was certainly true of Freud's. His friend Wilhelm Fliess was a Berlin nose-and-throat specialist who believed he could diagnose emotional disturbances by examining nasal passages. He believed men and women had monthly sexual cycles, 23 days for men, 28 for women. His conversation was so free-floating and unconsidered that he's sometimes called "a wild man."

In Freud biographies he's usually dismissed as a crackpot. But apparently it was his wildness and his eccentricities that Freud valued.

Fliess's chutzpah and meshugas were infectious. After they had been close for years, Freud wrote to him that "You have taught me that a bit of truth lurks behind every popular lunacy."

At one point Freud wrote: "My dear Wilhelm: You will not have any objection to my calling my next son Wilhelm! If he turns out to be a girl, she will be called Anna." At another he wrote, "Many thanks for your beautiful picture! It will get the place of honor on my desk, the place you hold in my friendship."

Fliess was just distant enough, and just unorthodox enough, to inspire confessions. Freud tells him his reaction to his father's recent death ("I now feel quite uprooted") and describes a breakthrough in

SIGMUND FREUD, 1938, FREUD MUSEUM, LONDON

his theory ("The barriers suddenly lifted, the veils dropped. Everything seemed to fall into place, the cogs meshed").

More often he confesses failure. Even as Freud enters his most productive years, he feels neglected and underrated. "I am isolated," he writes in 1896. He felt his reputation was such that people were avoiding him. "This year for the first time my consulting room is empty, for weeks on end I see no new faces." And then, "Today I learned that a colleague at the university declined to have me as a consultant, with the explanation that I could not be taken seriously." In 1900 *The Interpretation of Dreams* appears: "The reception of the book and the ensuing silence have again destroyed any budding relationship with my milieu."

As their friendship grew, Fliess's unhinged quality opened Freud's literary side. He saw something larger, something beyond medicine. Freud slowly turned himself into a storyteller as well as a doctor. Their friendship ended, apparently over a misunderstanding, but it left Freud with a larger vision of personal freedom.

More than a few readers of Freud's books have noticed that he was a writer of exceptional talent. Karl Popper and many other eminent commentators derided Freud's theories (they cannot be tested, therefore they are not science), and in recent years that opinion has gathered strength. Now it seems possible that the future will know him principally as a major figure in the history of literature.

J.G. Ballard has written, rightly, that "Freud was a born storyteller ... with a great imaginative writer's ability to explore the human heart through the unfolding drama of a strong confrontational narrative." He invented a master narrative and argued that we should understand that it applies to the whole human race, a magnificent example of literary chutzpah. Those who believed him, and even those who half-believed, learned from him to see their own inner lives as contested territory.

He would not have been altogether disappointed if posterity placed him permanently among respected authors. He often said that writers of fiction had taught him a great deal. He wrote to a fellow Viennese, Arthur Schnitzler, a brilliant playwright: "The impression has been borne in on me that you know through intuition – really from a delicate self-observation – everything that I have discovered in other people by laborious work." Occasionally he went so far as to analyze dreams found in a work of fiction, explaining: "Story-tellers are valuable allies, for they usually know many things that our academic wisdom does not even dream of.... they draw from sources we have not yet made accessible."

At certain points a reader senses that Freud is stepping outside the medical tradition and creating his own style through an unspoken alliance with literature.

He thinks in metaphors coloured by his sense of history, and he often draws images from warfare and politics. If a patient's development stalls, Freud compares it to an army held up for weeks by enemy resistance on a road that could be crossed swiftly in peacetime. He says the unconscious operates as a spy who infiltrates the "land." To do so, it must acquire a false passport, disguising its true identity. Dreams operate as "invading conquerors." Freud describes how the birth of a sibling leaves the elder child "dethroned."

How to define the id? Freud finds the ideal method, personalizing this force as he did so many others. He tells us the id can be rebuked, can be put in its place, but it will have its revenge. It's "the non-commissioned officer who accepts a reprimand from his superior in silence but vents his anger upon the first innocent private he happens to meet." This hard-to-forget parade-ground image brings the concept to life in all its rage and wayward retribution. His metaphors deepen and enrich the idea that every personality wars with itself. Has anyone else, acting in the name of science, made more inventive use of metaphor?

Freud's case histories are constructed according to a template familiar to readers of short fiction – especially Sherlock Holmes stories. Playfully, Freud likes to delay gratification, holding back the solution until the moment when its revelation will have the greatest impact.

One characteristic Freud shares with many fiction writers and poets is his ability to come down firmly and even vehemently (sometimes even unreasonably) on more than one side of the same question. He differs from almost all scientists in this sense; scientists can change their minds, but when they do they usually explain themselves, often in great detail, keeping in mind their reputations for consistency. Freud, on the other hand, was never afraid of self-con-tradition and rarely seemed even to notice it. There's little in his body of work that he doesn't contradict somewhere else.

On one specific issue, the art and practice of biography, his attitude resembled the famous dictum of a famous admirer of Freud, W. H. Auden. Over many years Auden said that he hoped no one would ever write his biography; he urged all of his friends to burn any letters of his that they had kept. (So far as we know, none did.) Auden said that a writer's life is in his work; everything else that could be told was extraneous. Yet he frequently reviewed biographies of other writers and apparently found them not only instructive but enjoyable. In 1969 he reviewed J. R. Ackerley's autobiography, *My Father and Myself*, with such engagement and brio that I recall key passages to this day.

When I asked Auden about this apparent conflict he replied that others could take it or leave it, but that was how he felt on the subject-a masterful poet's typically whimsical, and understandable, justification.

Freud found biographies so untrustworthy that he viewed the very process with profound scepticism. In his practice he learned that the intimate stories told about individuals, like the stories they tell themselves (and then tell biographers), hide the truth. He distrusted coherent, confident narrative. He argued that biographical truth is not to be had. "To be a biographer you must tie yourself up in lies, concealments, hypocrisies."

Even so, he included biographical data in his case histories and wrote books on Moses, Leonardo, and Michelangelo, all of them highly speculative. In the case of Leonardo, Freud was preposterously reckless: he wrote a psychoanalytic study based on his paintings. Today it is read for what it says about Freud, not for any truths about Leonardo. A quarter-century after his death, Freud appeared as co-author, with Ambassador William C. Bullitt, of a Woodrow Wilson biography, described by almost everyone who read it as a failure. These are relatively easygoing books, containing none of the self-conscious solemnity Freud affected when addressing the reader (and his fellow analysts) on points of psychoanalytic principle; perhaps they are late echoes of his free-ranging conversations with Fliess.

Biographers typically write as if delivering to readers a final and (they hope) irrefutable judgement on the book's subject; but of course no such judgement is available. Adam Phillips, the author of a brilliant study, *Becoming Freud: The Making of a Psychoanalyst* (2014), reminds us that Freud (aside from creating a story in which the author, while treating patients, realizes that he is a patient himself) worked a fundamental change in biography. He accomplished that because his theories were so persuasive that he made the discussion of any personality vastly more complicated than it had been. Freud licensed everyone, biographers and readers, to imagine complexities that would rarely have occurred to anyone before his time.

He taught us to raise painful and sometimes shameful issues that were traditionally ignored or neglected in biographies, above all issues grounded in family and sexuality. A biography of the late John Cheever, for instance, must now deal at length with his lethal alcoholism, his homosexuality, and his fractured family life, issues that would, in pre-Freudian days, be handled euphemistically if at all.

Today, after four or five generations of authors have absorbed Freudian theory, all biography is in a sense Freudian, even if the biographer affects to disdain his theories. This must be one reason biography (including film and TV versions) is more popular today than at any time in the past. It's commonplace for someone to say that we live in the age of biography and autobiography.

Among the many other accidental effects of Freud's writing is the steadily increasing popularity of paranoid belief in conspiracy. Freud taught us, as much as he taught us anything, that nothing on the surface is to be believed – there is usually a potentially discoverable lie at the heart of all human activity, especially family life. Many among us have transferred this into public life and drawn up largely imaginary tales of conspiracies that explain everything from Pearl Harbor to John Kennedy's death to the 9/11 massacre.

> *His imagination was so crowded with those battles, enchant-*
> *ments, adventures, amorous thoughts, and other whimsies which*
> *he had read of in romances that his fancy changed every-*
> *thing he saw into what he desired to see;*
> *and he could not conceive that the dust was only raised by*

two large flocks of sheep. He was positive that they were two armies....

Don Quixote, the greatest book-length fantasy in Western literature, was, all his life, Freud's favourite book. As a schoolboy he taught himself Spanish so that he could read it as Cervantes wrote it. He and a friend who shared the book's attraction invented Spanish names for themselves and for a while exchanged letters commenting, Cervantes-style, on their activities.

Open *Don Quixote* at random and you discover that it's one of those rare masterpieces that discloses its meaning on any page. Of course it is a comedy of self-delusion and a satire on the foolishness that an excessive conscience can engender. In the passage quoted, Don Quixote goes on to say that he and Sancho Panza must choose between the two armies: "What shall we do but assist the weak and the injured side?"

While knowing nothing, he remains confident that as a good knight, whose heart is pure, he will prove his virtue and also emerge triumphant, as in so many novels he's read. In other words, the Don is fiction's victim. At its core *Don Quixote* is a book about books; its persistent theme is the self-righteousness peddled by hack literature.

Adam Phillips explains that Freud liked to think of himself as the solid, faithful but honest Sancho Panza rather than the addled Don Quixote. But, Phillips goes on, they were inextricable. They act out a story of two men and what they do together, "one of them dominated to the point of madness by a fictional past."

Auden's memorial poem on Freud says that he taught the world to look back with no false regrets.

He wasn't clever at all: he merely told
the unhappy Present to recite the Past.

And in the process told humanity a new story.

The Artist as Scoundrel

ROBERT FROST THROWING STONES IN GLOUCESTER, ENGLAND, 1957. GETTY IMAGES

In his conversation as much as in his prose, John Cheever embodied the calm, lucid, sophisticated style developed by the *New Yorker*, the magazine where, for four decades or so, thousands of admirers read his stories. No one, in fact, was more *New Yorker*ish than he. But in retrospect it's clear that his manner was a fraud. And because he wanted to give posterity an honest version of his life, he left behind his diaries, 30 volumes of them, so that we who outlived him could know the ugly truth.

The ugly truth has a way of eventually becoming clear to many of us who find ourselves emotionally drawn to the work of certain writers, painters, and musicians. It is their art we love, but we eventually want to know about their lives; and often that knowledge creates severe disappointment.

The pious response to this experience is simple enough: the art matters, not the life. The life should be ignored except by those hopelessly addicted to gossip. Forget what we can read about Charles Dickens, for example. Love his books, forget the rest.

But, human curiosity being what it is, we want to know what lies behind the art. So in 2012, as the English-speaking world celebrated the 200th birthday of its greatest novelist, books and articles and TV shows about Dickens dwelled on, among other matters, the appalling aspects of his private life. We had many opportunities to read about his swinish treatment of his wife, and it was written often that he was nearly as bad a parent as his own parents were, though in a different way. But how could this be true of Dickens, a man (we readers know for sure) of consummate humanity, a man equipped with a generous spirit he exhibited in book after book?

John Cheever presents a similar instance, though of course on a lesser historical scale. His life was painful and chaotic. Cheever's characters often burned with indignation or resentment or unresolved yearnings; yet their fury rarely swept over its banks, as Cheever's own did. Often he drank from breakfast till bedtime, and he sometimes became so drunk that he exploded in violence. A bad husband, a bad father, and an extensive heterosexual adulterer, he was also a passionate homosexual and believed that this last aspect of his life particularly shamed him. He routinely falsified his background, giving himself a family history of some distinction and elegance that was more fanciful than real – in the end he regarded himself as "a cheap social climber, an imitation gentleman."

As the uncomfortable facts about his life began to appear, in the mid-1980s, I was among the devoted readers of Cheever who were startled. Mordecai Richler, who knew and liked him, was appalled as well as shocked by the revelations that appeared in *Home Before Dark*, a memoir his daughter Susan Cheever wrote in 1984, just two years after her father died. Richler thought it indecent that the squalor and misery of Cheever's life should be brought to light. He wanted not to know it. So, in a sense, did I.

We should not have been particularly surprised. As readers of biographies and reviews of biographies, as friends or acquaintances of certain artists, we had been through all this before. In fact, disillusionment over the lives of cultural giants has by now become a commonplace aspect of studying cultural history.

According to Patrick French's biography of V. S. Naipaul, *The World Is What It Is*, the 2001 winner of the Nobel Prize monstrously mistreated both his first wife and his long-time mistress, out of a bottomless narcissism that allowed no room for the feelings of anyone but himself. And French was Naipaul's own choice as a biographer. Much of the book's material came directly from Naipaul.

It's argued sometimes that in his case the work determined the nature of the man. As a writer he grew a tough carapace. He made himself strong enough to disdain any hint of compromise in the way he judged the characters in his books, including the characters partly based on himself. Nor was he bothered, in the non-fiction books, by any desire to show himself tolerant of other races and other faiths. The fact that he was often called a brown-skinned racist only proved to him the banality of arguments about colour. One admirer of Naipaul's writing, Hilary Spurling, wrote: "The harsh emotional honesty that made him as a writer destroyed him as a man."

However we explain it, this phenomenon creates certain puzzles about human personality. Aspects of it may occasionally be comic, but it is ultimately appalling, a kind of scandal that repeats itself endlessly and yet never quite loses its ability to shock. Many of us, when we are young, imagine that those whose work we admire will themselves be admirable. Even in later years we are reluctant to surrender this notion. It accompanies many of us far into our adult life.

Frank Lloyd Wright, when in the midst of a public scandal, gave a press conference to explain that he was a genius, and geniuses were not subject to the codes that govern non-geniuses. I have known more than a few artists who, without exactly making a credible claim to genius (much as they would like to), believe in all apparent sincerity that by simply devoting their lives to art they have won permanent forgiveness for all conceivable moral infractions.

The life of Picasso offers a thousand reasons for disillusionment.

He was not so gauche as to state his belief that genius gave him unlimited licence to do as he pleased; he simply did it and never looked back. Picasso used each successive woman in his life as both mistress and model until he exhausted her value; he then moved on to a new woman. If children appeared they were subject to a unique form of emotional brutality: he adored them as babies and small children but (as one of his mistresses testified at some length) lost interest as soon as they reached puberty.

Then he forgot they existed. He never explained this practice; it was just what he felt like doing, and so he did it automatically. It is hard to read a biography of him without thinking of him as a scoundrel. But then, Stan Getz, admired by two generations of jazz lovers as a sophisticated tenor saxophone soloist and a man of infinite harmonic inventiveness, was also known to his colleagues as a chronic wife-beater and an addict who would do anything to feed his heroin habit. Miles Davis, the most impressive trumpet player of his generation, was a cruel boor to everyone but a few intimates. Both Getz and Davis enjoyed, at their peak, the very highest status in the jazz world.

How can we think about this disquieting but also undeniable collection of abnormalities among the creative classes? Consider the spectacular case of Robert Frost.

One night in the 1930s Archibald MacLeish was reading his poetry at the Bread Loaf Conference in Middlebury, Vermont. Robert Frost was there, but he was not paying attention to the reading. He

was interrupting, making loud comments, trying to attract
attention. He settled on an ideal way to have everyone notice him.
He struck a match and set a few pieces of paper on fire. Putting
out the blaze made Frost the centre of attention and destroyed
MacLeish's moment.

That was too much for Bernard DeVoto, an excellent critic and journalist. He knew already, as did everyone else present, that Frost was
a better poet than MacLeish. (An opinion literary history has amply
confirmed.) He also knew that Frost had often treated lesser poets
in this way, apparently to make sure everyone knew his own status.
DeVoto felt he could no longer remain silent. He was compelled to
state what everyone knew but no one had ever managed to say aloud:
"You're a good poet, Robert, but you're a bad man." He determined
never to speak to him again. But Frost eventually found a furtive way
of replying. A few years later DeVoto heard that Frost was telling lies
about him: "DeVoto, you know, has been under the care of a psychia-
trist, who has told him that I am not good for him, that if he is ever to
succeed, he must not cultivate my company: I am too strong for him
and have a bad effect on him."

As Frost grew old, there were no signs that he was showing, any-
where outside his poems, even a touch of wisdom. What grew in his
late decades was obsessive vanity; that was the Frost poets knew at
Bread Loaf and other venues. The rest of the United States, with the
help of a few genial features in the newspapers, viewed him as a lovable curmudgeon, a national grandpa, full of homely wisdom. By the
time he read a poem at John Kennedy's inauguration in 1961 he was an
emblem of American national spirit. When he died two years later, at
the age of 89, he was mourned as a great poet and a grand old man.

The biographies that followed in the 1970s told a different story.
He was a wretched husband and father, a tyrant in personal and
professional relations, jealous and vindictive. Also a chronic liar. He
claimed to come from poverty and reported that his evil grandfather
stole his money. In truth, his grandfather left him enough money to
support him as a poet for many years.

Frost was the chief example chosen by the late Wayne C. Booth, a
distinguished literary scholar and the inventor over 50 years ago of

the term "unreliable narrator," when he gave some serious thought to the question of the morals that lie behind masterpieces. In a lecture at the University of Chicago in 2000, he suggested that there was a good deal of hypocrisy in the way artists present themselves to the public. But hypocrisy of this kind is not evil; it may be a positive good. He called it "hypocrisy upward."

He defined it as the effort to create a work that implies its author possesses greater wisdom than the flesh-and-blood human. Booth imagined the author choosing a better self from his repertoire of personalities. "Our lives would be cursed if writers did not practice such hypocrisy. We need those created, somewhat faked models. We are... blessed when skilful authors perform selves superior to their everyday, warts-laden selves."

He noted that Denis Donoghue, accurately summarizing two biographies in the *New York Review of Books*, described Frost as "an appalling man, petty, vindictive, a dreadful husband and parent ... a monster, a man of systematic cruelty."

Booth invited us to distinguish between the created self presented by the artist in poetry or some other art and the deplorable individual who appears in the biographies. The created Robert Frost, for instance, is not only as real as the flesh-and-blood sinner, "he is in one sense more real, and of course far more influential. In creating him, Frost has created a version of his self not only that he likes better but also that elevates his world and mine. Just think how impoverished our lives would be without such elevations – whether we call them hypocritical or not."

In fact, Booth said, he had found his admiration for Frost the poet actually rising slightly as he learned some contemptible details about the everyday Frost. "How could a man plagued with such faults and miseries produce such beautiful, moving poetry?" Frost aspired to be, and succeeded in becoming, "a realer, truer, more genuine version than the one who was sometimes cruel to his wife and children."

Booth's way of analyzing this issue leaves us where we most want to be: we can wholeheartedly embrace the art while comprehending the nature of the life. Only one other statement on this subject impresses me more, and it comes from Charles Dickens. Interviewed in 1862 by a young admirer, Fyodor Dostoevsky, Dickens explained that all the good, simple people in his novels are what he wanted to have been, and his villains were what he sometimes found himself to be. Dostoevsky wrote: "There were two people in him, he told me: one who feels as he ought to feel and one who feels the opposite. From the one who feels the opposite I make my evil characters, from the one who feels as a man ought to feel, I try to live my life."

In recent years those lines have often been quoted, including by me, and they appear in two biographies of Dickens, including the one by Claire Tomalin, *Charles Dickens: A Life* (2011). Tomalin calls this passage "amazing," mainly because it shows Dickens saying what anybody familiar with his work and his life has always intuited. "It is as though with Dostoevsky he could drop the appearance of perfect virtue he felt he had to keep up before the English public." Tomalin thinks it the most profound statement he made about his inner life. Agreed, but unfortunately the authenticity of the story, and the letter in which Dostoevsky recounted it, have lately been questioned. I for one hope it survives the scrutiny of the scholars and continues to demonstrate that Dickens, whose wonderfully broad intelligence comprehended so much, understood even the most crucial contradictions in his own personality.

Under the Spell of the Tango

When I was a boy, Hollywood musical comedies taught me that tango was a kind of joke, an over-the-top, tempestuous exhibition of feigned emotion. Often a movie would contain a brief tango performance inserted purely for comic effect. Typically, the male dancer would miss his cue and hurl his partner violently across the room, or (in one film I remember) into a swimming pool. In retrospect the cultural meaning of those scenes is clear: by the middle of the last century tango had become (in North American eyes) so outlandishly passionate that it could be dealt with only through parody and burlesque.

The people who run El Querandí, one of many supper tango clubs in Buenos Aires, are only too aware of this derisive tradition. They know it has affected many South Americans (the largest part of their clientele) as well as North Americans and Europeans. Before beginning its big show of the evening, El Querandí projects a montage of scenes from old movies in which the stylized passion of the tango is the butt of the joke. When I was there about ten years ago they ran a delightful piece by Laurel and Hardy, another by Chaplin, and a glimpse of Valentino in action – he being, in the eyes of tango aficionados, the definition of tango as unintentional parody.

That done, El Querandí set about the task of demonstrating how tango should be performed – seriously, ardently, with a sense of history and a commitment to the art. But of course this still involved displaying some of the often-parodied elements as well as the originality and grace of the dancers, singers, and musicians.

The women wore net stockings, transparent gowns, and facial expressions as blank as runway models. Male dancers, of course, wore fedoras pulled down over their also blank faces. Every year the fedora comes closer to extinction, and it occurred to me several times during my visit to Buenos Aires that perhaps male tango dancers would someday be the last fedora-wearers on earth. (But at this point in history, a national fedora shortage in Argentina would paralyze the art of tango.)

In the first dance of the evening a knife appeared briefly in a male dancer's hand, as if in tribute to the primitive beginnings of tango (in the 1880s or 1890s) among the pimps, prostitutes, and sex-starved

SHEET MUSIC ILLUSTRATION BY FABIEN LORIS, 1926

gauchos, in from the pampas to make love and trouble in Buenos
Aires. That dance, and some of those that followed during the evening, achieved a fierceness that hinted at the dark appeal Jorge Luis
Borges always found in the stories of fearless and sometimes mur-
derous gauchos. Tango has always carried an overtone of menace.

Those who listen only occasionally to tango music miss its diver-
sity of expression, the subtle shadings of its narrative. Tango works
within a limited emotional range, true, but so does a fugue or a
Broadway ballad. It is only when confronted by a whole evening of
dancers and singers that one understands the multiplicity of attitudes they strike and the subtle pacing of their performances. I had
heard about the millions of people enthralled by tango (I had also
seen Buenos Aires record stores where half the CDs were tango music) but until visiting El Querandí I didn't understand how it draws
the audience into its special ambit.

Once engaged, the audience begins to realize that the energy depends on swift mood changes in the stories that the dancers perform
symbolically. These miniplots are never more than fragmentary,
glimpsed out of the corner of the mind's eye, like the lyrics of Paul
Simon songs. But their existence transforms the tango into drama as
much as dance. The performers slowly unfold a story, often involv-
ing a hint of erotic history. As it develops they depict acceptance,
then rejection, then perhaps acceptance again.

Angry indecision is the essence of the characters they are playing.
Often disillusionment becomes part of the narrative, and sometimes
contempt. Each character is aware at every moment of potential
betrayal. A compelling sexuality provides the fundamental mood,
never more powerfully felt than when the dancers pull back from
each other's touch. Disappointment is never more than two bars
away. Tango is a choreographed seduction with no guarantee that it
will achieve its goal.

It requires athletic skill, but these athletes must never show even a
hint of strain. They dance their complicated figures, legs gracefully
entwined, as if there were nothing else that a sensible person should
be doing at this moment. They tell their anecdotes without words,
of course, but also without facial expression. They relax their masks

only to indicate irony or disdain, but never anything approaching happiness. Tango is melodrama yearning to be tragedy. It is saturated with self-pity. Its tone is bathos raised, by the compressed intensity of its performers, to the level of art.

Over a century or so, tango has established itself as the most cherished art form of Argentina and the special pride of Buenos Aires, where it was born. Buenos Aires is to tango what New Orleans is to jazz;' the parallels are undeniable. Both cities grew up as world ports with heterogeneous populations, and in both places danger plays a large part in local mythology. In each city an art form sprang to life in bordellos, patronized by (sometimes performed by) criminals. In both cases art followed the same course, from whorehouse entertainment to high-class nightclubs to concert halls. Finally it arrived in the universities, as a subject of musicological and historical study. And tango, like jazz, has often been the subject of arguments over "authenticity." With tango it comes down, in effect, to a question of ownership. Does tango uniquely express the spirit of Buenos Aires people, the *porteños*, a spirit that others can't begin to understand or appreciate? Or is it music and dance that can be universally loved?

In both Buenos Aires and New Orleans a once-scorned popular form has become the city's signature, its main attraction, and its consolation in times of trouble. Tango and jazz alike are advertisements for the achievements of upward mobility – a process that began with tango just before the First World War, when Argentinian dancers suddenly became popular from Paris to St Petersburg, an achievement that eventually impressed all classes back home in Argentina.

Where New Orleans music was profoundly shaped by slavery, tango grew out of the sense of displacement produced by immigration (from Italy, Germany, and several other countries) combined with poverty. It was born, writes Erin Manning of Concordia University in *Politics of Touch: Sense, Movement, Sovereignty* (2006), "of disillusionment and disorientation." It became the art of "immigrants searching for a vocabulary to express their place-less-ness in their new country." And finding it, for the most part, in the failures of romantic love.

Academic critics point out that tango is an art of consolation, a
point that becomes clear when we hear in tango lyrics the genuine
emotion lying behind the formalized art. Marta Savigliano of the
University of California, in *Tango and the Political Economy of Passion*
(1995), declares that "Tangos are spectacular confessions. They are
public displays of intimate miseries, shameful behaviours, and un-
justifiable attitudes," the expressions of the private, personal world
but addressed to the public world.

An underappreciated 2002 movie, *Assassination Tango*, presented
this art form as a kind of therapy for a yearning soul. Robert Duvall
– the writer, director, and star – plays an American hit man sent to
Buenos Aires to assassinate a general. Waiting for his victim to arrive
in town, he wanders into a dance club and finds himself attracted
to a tango dancer. She agrees to his request that she give him tango
lessons. We soon understand that he's a man exiled from himself,
unable to see his way out of a life that is at once appalling and boring.
His emotions are in chaos, which is where tango comes in. It provides
a structure, a framework for his sense of desolation. Duvall clearly
focuses on the sharply limited emotional promise of tango. It doesn't
cure melancholy and despair, but it provides a way to endure it.

Tango dancers shade the fables they tell with a certain irony, even
if they express it only through a raised eyebrow. Tango singers, on
the other hand, barely acknowledge that irony exists. They are far
too busy mourning. It is their central role in Argentine culture, a
serious business. One of the hit songs of Roberto Goyeneche (1926-
1994), a singer of some eminence, has a title that translates as "The
Last Drink of the Night" and a climactic line that says "life is an absurd wound." That's the tango-singer philosophy compressed into
five words. There is no such thing as an unwounded tango singer.

In the world of tango lyrics, things are always bad and will probably get worse before they become really terrible. More than that,
there's nothing that can be done about it. Tango singers mainly tell
us love stories, but these are also allegories. A lament for lost love
serves as a masked lament for the public fate of Argentina. So many
terrible things have happened to Argentina, most of them political,
that they seem to many Argentinians inevitable. In the non-polit-

ical classes, betrayed so often by the politicians, resignation is the common response. Donald S. Castro, in *The Argentine Tango as Social History* (1991), points out that tango lyrics routinely take a passive view of misfortune: while expressing the singer's sorrows, they offer little hope of salvation. "Misfortune is to be suffered as a normal part of life, not avoided."

Given that attitude, tango from the beginning has been an art form ready to embrace and celebrate martyrdom. The perfect martyr was created on June 24, 1935, when two aircraft collided in Medellin, Colombia, one of them containing the most popular of all tango singers, Carlos Gardel. He had recorded about 1,000 songs and appeared in a long series of films. He had many imitators and millions of admirers, in Europe and the US as well as South America. In the first three months of his visit to France in 1928, he sold 70,000 records.

Donald Castro says his death ended an era in Argentine popular music but began a new period for Gardel as the prime symbol of Buenos Aires and its people.

Since then he has grown steadily more famous and more admired; according to a popular saying, his singing continues to improve. Castro claims he's "a cultural symbol to fill a political leadership vacuum," his image rising with each failure of the political class. Nationalism also played into his legend. Argentinians, having felt the lack of their own culture and often complaining about European cultural domination, were delighted to see Gardel creating Argentina's own form of expression.

In the popular culture of the world no other reputation has lasted as long as Gardel's. Elvis Presley's and John Lennon's are similar but they have been dead for just four decades. Gardel has been in the grave for over eight decades, getting on for four generations, and yet remains a major figure on the Buenos Aires cityscape. It is as if North Americans were to make a permanent hero of Rudy Vallée or another performer from the 1920s or 1930s. Stars of that generation, the great figures from the early days of radio and recordings, have disappeared from the imagination, unless (like Bing Crosby and Louis Armstrong) they remained active well into the second half of the twentieth century, renewing their audience by their presence.

In Gardel's singing we hear, across all this time, an urgency, an I-will-be-heard determination. There are no casual, easygoing Gardel records, so far as I know. His style always implies that something vital is at stake. Much of his permanent appeal rests on the way he managed to braid together the tango and his own voice, as if one could not exist without the other. His personality was another crucial factor. He was handsome, masculine, successful, yet somehow vulnerable and often (in his songs) defeated. In Gardel songs there's one recurrent character: a woman who betrays her lover and then leaves him. A typical line runs, "Tell me dear girl, what have you/done with my poor heart?" Defeat is his constant theme.

Gardel never married, but there were public hints of various liaisons, always clouded in mystery. There was mystery surrounding his birth, too. In his youth he claimed Tacuarembo, Uruguay, as his birthplace, apparently to indicate he was part of the local scene. (Today the football team in San Carlos, Uruguay, is called the Club Carlos Gardel.) In fact, that was the birthplace on the passport he carried at the time of his death. Biographers, however, have decided that he was born in France in 1890 and registered as Charles Romuald Gardes by the Toulouse authorities. No father was named. His mother, Berthe Gardes, brought him to Argentina as an infant and he grew so dedicated to his new home that when asked about his birth he would sometimes say that he was born in Buenos Aires, at the age of two.

Berthe Gardes settled in the Abasto district, then a market area like Les Halles in Paris, where she lived by ironing clothes in a cleaning store. In adolescence her son became a street singer, then worked in bars and restaurants, his supple baritone giving everything he sang an air of dramatic romance. By 1910 he had taken the name Gardel, which sounded more local, and changed Charles to Carlos. In 1917 his first tango record opened a new era in popular song and set the tone of his career – *Mi noche triste* ("My Sad Night").

Today the Abasto neighbourhood has a Carlos Gardel subway station, a Carlos Gardel street, three giant murals of his face on the exteriors of buildings, a life-size bronze statue, and the Museo Casa Carlos Gardel, installed in a little house where he once lived.

On the fiftieth anniversary of his death, in 1985, a mass newspaper ran a supplement headed "Carlos Gardel: A Half-Century of Eternal Greatness." Today the national music awards are called Los Premios Gardel. Walking near the San Telmo market, where people often tango in the streets, I saw a man in a T-shirt that said "Gardel Lives."

During half-time at a major professional football game, the scoreboard interrupted the flow of TV-style advertising with an excerpt from a black-and-white film. It showed two men in fedoras talking at the rail during a horse race. One of them began singing, about good fortune and bad fortune. It was Carlos Gardel. Hundreds of young football fans in the crowd stood swaying and singing along with him. In Buenos Aires you are never far from tango, which means you are never far from Carlos Gardel.

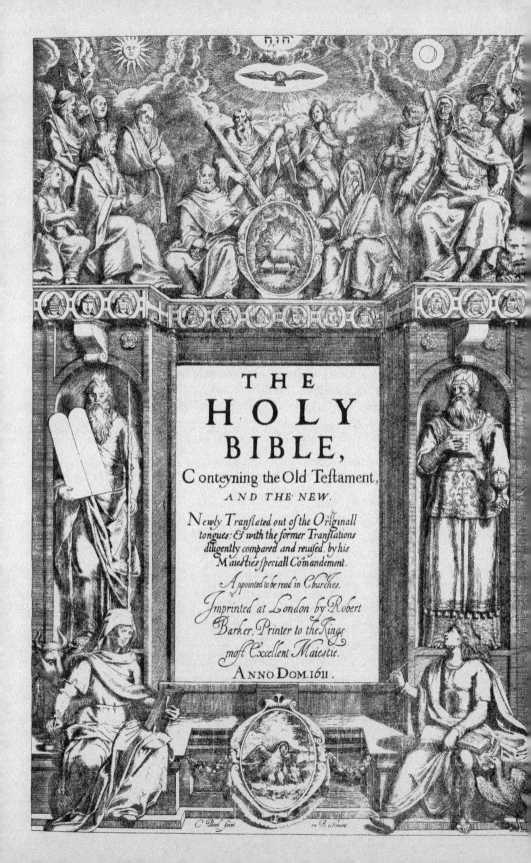

THE
HOLY
BIBLE,

C onteyning the Old Testament,

AND THE NEW.

Newly Translated out of the Originall
tongues: & with the former Translations
diligently compared and reuised, by his
Maiesties speciall Comandement.

Appointed to be read in Churches.

Imprinted at London by Robert
Barker, Printer to the Kings
most Excellent Maiestie.

ANNO DOM. 1611.

C. Boel fecit in Richmont

Reading The Bible
Through a Glass Darkly

W hen I take a few moments to read in the King James Version the stirring, poetic and sweetly reasonable wisdom of Ecclesiastes, or the often disagreeable but brilliantly pronounced theology of St Paul, I feel, for a moment, both awkward and self-conscious. I'm sure I'm not alone. Every unbeliever who spends time reading the seventeenth-century English version of the Bible, the one we familiarly call the KJV, must at times feel like a kind of intruder. There's something slightly perverse in the private, impious and altogether worldly way we adopt, as if it were our own possession, a book for which millions of people fought and died and which many more embraced as their lifelong guide to existence. Those who set down the text of the KJV, and those who spent generations carefully spreading it through the English-speaking world, did not intend it for such as we.

The KJV harbours a multitude of qualities that turn writing into art. Its hundreds of pages are filled with metaphors, symbols, analogies, rhetorical speech, and tribal sagas, braided into a long and rewarding series of mythologies. But what right have we to call it literature when it was first of all something quite different – and, in a sense, more serious? When new editions of the Bible appear, usually for the purpose of clarifying scripture and sorting out mistakes made in the KJV, what right have we to demean these earnest projects by comparing them with the KJV?

Why did Christopher Hitchens (that eminent atheist) feel entitled to brush aside "the flat banality of the so-called New English Bible"? In 2003, reviewing *God's Secretaries: The Making of the King James Bible* by Adam Nicolson, he said that in revising the Bible these "committees of English and American Protestantism came together and threw a pearl away richer than all their tribe," the KJV. He was taking his stand as a friend of literature, grateful to organized Christianity for giving him the KJV and prepared to defend its virtues against any inferior replacement.

Literary people have often protested against offences committed by biblical scholars in the interests of religious understanding. Consider a famous passage from 1 Corinthians: "When I was a child, I spake as a child, I understood as a child, I thought as a child.

But when I became a man, I put away childish things. For now we see through a glass, darkly." In 1961 the New English Bible put it this way: "When I was a child, my speech, my outlook, and my thoughts were childish. When I grew up, I had finished with childish things. Now we see only puzzling reflections in a mirror."

Dwight Macdonald, a sharp-eyed American essayist and a KJV partisan, said that coming upon those words was like finding a parking lot where a great church once stood. In the seventeenth century the KJV translators seem to have decided that St Paul's Greek meant we all, even as adults, can see life (this life or the next one) at best partially. But they may have had other meanings in mind. When they were doing their work, from 1604 to 1611, "darkly" could be a synonym for secretly, sombrely, mysteriously, dimly – or gloomy. Like many KJV passages, that brief translation has enjoyed a spectacular secondary career on the farther shores of modern culture. Perhaps because it seems to our minds both attractive and ambiguous, "Through a Glass Darkly" has become the title of at least two rock albums, at least four TV episodes, a chamber symphony, a mystery story by Donna Leon, an American priest's book on US policy in Guatemala, a report on alcohol from the British Methodist Church, an Ingmar Bergman film – and a poem by General George Patton. Perhaps St Paul was in fact referring to the relatively primitive mirrors of his time; perhaps the 1961 scholars felt they were putting things right, but in the last fifty years "puzzling reflections in a mirror" has made no similar impact on anyone's imagination.

The KJV is the most famous and perhaps the only masterpiece produced by a committee. And not a small committee. The team of translators encompassed six "companies," each with nine men, plus a few others who helped out occasionally. Having performed this magnificent service, most of them then stepped back into the shadows; few ever became known, beyond their own time in history, for anything else. Only one, Lancelot Andrewes, developed a reputation that reached into the twentieth century. He was a bishop, a prodigiously talented linguist, a wily politician, a famous preacher, and a supporter of the divine right of kings. In 1928 T.S. Eliot wrote a book about his prose. Kurt Vonnegut, in his autobiographical novel

Timequake (1997), called Andrewes "the greatest writer in the English language" and credited him with translating the Twenty-third Psalm. Andrewes headed the team that translated the first twelve books of the Hebrew Bible (Genesis to 2 Kings) and acted as general editor of the whole project.

He and his colleagues worked with unbelievable speed. In just seven years the KJV progressed from idea stage to printed copies. King James was impatient to see it. The KJV was in essence his shrewd and far-sighted political strategy. His motto was "Blessed are the Peacemakers," and he imagined all of England worshipping in just the same way. An authoritative Bible would create unity within the English church and marginalize both Catholics who wanted to return to Rome and Protestants whose ideas were often dangerously extreme.

For the future of our language it was a piece of pure luck that the monarchy required a new version of the Bible just when the speaking and writing of English was in its richest, most expansive, and most adventurous phase. The growing popularity of printing and the high ambitions of the Elizabethan era coincided with, and helped produce, a moment like no other in the development of English. The biblical translation moved toward completion as the last plays of Shakespeare (so far as scholarship can tell us) were being written, among them *King Lear* and *The Tempest*.

Another factor makes the KJV's generally high literary quality even more surprising: in modern terms it was partly a rewrite job. Earlier translations, by William Tyndale, Miles Coverdale, and others, were considered inadequate or theologically unsound. Still, parts of them could be used. So the KJV had 60-some scholars who were equipped to argue with each other and at the same time had the right to haggle over their various views of the work of their predecessors. We know little of their private meetings (at which they read their translations aloud to each other, awaiting comments), but my guess is that Andrewes was the most accomplished committee chairman in history.

In the end about six-tenths of the passages in the KJV were taken in part from earlier translations. On 111 occasions the team used Cov-

erdale's formulation, "three score years and ten," rather than
the simple "seventy" that appeared in Hebrew. This was the cadence
that Abraham Lincoln borrowed for the opening of the Gettysburg
Address, "Four score and seven years ago ..." He wanted to give
weight to his words and ascend at a measured pace toward his climax – a technique that has since been lost by orators. As on a million
other occasions, KJV phrasing did the job. Lincoln was always conscious of what he called, in his first inaugural address, "The mystic
chords of memory." More than any other statesman in history, he
reflected in his public words his careful reading of the Bible.

KJV usage can sometimes baffle us, but just as often it surprises us
by how close it seems to our own twenty-first-century way of speaking and thinking. The reason, of course, is that it installed in our
language a buzzing swarm of metaphors that live in conversation
to this moment. This is the ultimate proof of its success: it reached
out from the churches and schools and invaded the lives of English
speakers everywhere. Whether we have read it or not, we all live it.
Many of the words that routinely tumble out of our mouths were put
there by the KJV translators. The Old Testament (or Hebrew Bible)
has told us about moving from strength to strength, going like a
lamb to slaughter, falling on our faces – and, appropriately, putting words in the mouths of others. It teaches us the metaphorical
meaning of sour grapes and reminds us that pride goeth before a fall.
The New Testament instructs us in the value of the salt of the earth
and on giving up the ghost. It describes the tragedy of a thorn in the
flesh, and reminds us of the necessity of dealing with the powers
that be.

Alister McGrath, who wrote *In the Beginning: The Story of the King
James Bible* (2001), tried to capture in a sentence the effect that the
KJV has had on artists over the last four centuries: "Without the
King James Bible, there would have been no *Paradise Lost*, no *Pilgrim's
Progress*, no Handel's *Messiah*, no Negro spirituals, and no Gettysburg
address." The reference to spirituals evokes a culture of slavery and
liberation. The Hebrew Bible's eloquent account of oppressed Jews
in Egypt gave slaves stolen from Africa a language of hope. Later it
provided Martin Luther King Jr with the cadences that made him the

great American orator of his century.

Robert Alter's study, *Pen of Iron: American Prose and the King James Bible* (2010), will add to almost anyone's pleasure in the KJV. It describes the several literary patterns that Americans have borrowed from the KJV but focuses on one, paratactic sentence structure. This is the format that assembles a series of facts or events side by side, linking them only by a conjunction, usually "and." The Book of Job, for instance, begins: "There was a man in the land of Uz, whose name was Job; and that man was perfect and upright, and one that feared God, and eschewed evil." In Hebrews a similar style appears: "For ye are not come unto the mount that might be touched, and that burned with fire, nor unto blackness, and darkness, and tempest. And the sound of a trumpet, and the voice of words.... And so terrible was the sight."

As Alter says, "The artfulness of biblical parataxis is precisely in its refusal to spell out causal connections, to interpret the reported data for us." *Moby-Dick* uses parataxis when Melville's narrator says: "The old craft dived deep in the green seas, and sent the shivering frost all over her, and the winds howled, and the cordage rang ..." A century later Alter finds Saul Bellow using his own intricate version of parataxis in *Seize the Day* (1956):

> Wilhelm respected the truth, but he could lie and one of the things he lied often about was his education. He said he was an alumnus of Penn State; in fact he had left school before his sophomore year was finished. His sister Catherine had a B.S. degree. Wilhelm's late mother was a graduate of Bryn Mawr. He was the only member of the family who had no education. This was another sore point. His father was ashamed of him.

Framed as a list, Tommy Wilhelm's inadequacies startle us with the cumulative weight of his self-accusation,

A striking example of parataxis that Alter doesn't mention is *Underworld* (1997), by Don DeLillo, which many critics have called the best American novel of recent decades. It's the sort of epic that covers several American decades, brings on Frank Sinatra and

J. Edgar Hoover for cameos, defines a great problem in American life (waste disposal, in this case), and frequently embarks on flights of poetic fancy. In this case the vehicle for these flights is biblical parataxis; and it works as well for DeLillo as it did for Melville.

DeLillo sets down the memories of a 1970s conceptual artist who spends her time painting junked warplanes in lush colours. We learn about her teenage visit to Manhattan with her mother:

> *And they stood outside a skyscraper on Fifth Avenue, it was probably 1934 and the Japanese were entrenched in Manchuria and they looked straight up the face of the building and walked through the polished lobby and it was the Fred F French Building, which intrigued the girls because who on earth was Fred F French, and Klara's mother ... did not have a clue to the identity of Fred F French, and this intrigued the girls even more ...*

Parataxis was used in the KJV to approximate the original biblical languages and give rhetorical force to a story. In DeLillo it reproduces a period-evoking stream of consciousness.

In childhood I belonged to no church, and I don't recall the appearance of a Bible in our family home, or for that matter any discussion of religion. My introduction to scripture was in public school, where of course it is now forbidden. We began every morning, hard as this is to believe in 2010, with a brief reading from the Bible. This was my fragmentary introduction to the KJV, which I began to appreciate only later and only as a part of literature.

I was impressed when I read somewhere that the KJV, more than any other book, had impressed Ernest Hemingway and shaped his style. By then, aged 13 or so, I yearned to imitate him and was just slightly disturbed to discover that he, too, had at some point imitated earlier writing. Still, I was fascinated to learn that the title of his first famous book, *The Sun Also Rises*, came from Ecclesiastes.

For much of its history, knowing the KJV was a sign of literacy. In fact, knowing how to read it was for many people, in more innocent times, a major if not the only reason for acquiring literacy. In millions of homes it was the only book, the centre of private education, the way for an isolated rural family to develop a perspective on the world and morality.

I pitied such people when I first read about them and then met a few. Later I envied them. Their form of literacy, wherever they pursued it, at least had a rich beginning. Today, most of the old KJV audience has died off. Later and inferior Bibles replaced it and then, through much of industrial society, religion lost its appeal and Bible study seemed increasingly irrelevant. When we use biblical language today we do so mostly by accident. Few of us quote the Bible and would be considered eccentric if we did. I think that the uneasiness that sometimes creeps up on me when I look into the KJV derives from a misunderstanding rooted, again, in boyhood.

I saw religion, churches, and Bibles as entirely interdependent, the related departments of the same enterprise. I imagined that in some sense the Protestant churches actually owned the Bible. That notion, if ever true, has long ceased to have meaning. Today, since few believers have need of the KJV, those who continue to cherish it are the literary people. Seventy-some years ago W.H. Auden disdained "those who read the Bible for its prose," implying that there were more serious reasons. Today, like it or not, a kind of elevated pleasure is the central reason for valuing the KJV. Today, everyone who cares about English shares the ownership of it. Everyone who cares about English is also responsible for its future.

To Live as a Legend

IGOR GOUZENKO AFTER TORONTO COURT APPEARANCE JUNE 1975. GLOBE AND MAIL

I dentity theft, as we read about it in the newspapers, usually involves acquiring, through on-line trickery, enough information to raid a bank account. This seems a petty, small-minded crime, though no doubt it will one day be classified as Grand Theft Digital. It's executed by people who have mastered better-than-average computer skills but aren't interested in legitimate jobs. As a covert means of obtaining money, it must be among the meanest.

Another kind of blurred and borrowed identity demands broader attention: the underground man, bearing fake documents, equipped with a life story built on lies. He (this character is usually male) carries an aura that fires the public imagination and inspires popular fiction, no matter how grubby the reality of his situation. John le Carré, in his espionage thrillers, popularized the term "legend," meaning the professionally concocted life story used by a spy in a clandestine role. "Legend" evokes dignity. It implies a shift from commonplace dissimulation into the realm of ancient fable. It moves a military decision, or even a con man's scheme, beyond banal falsehood and onto the more exalted ground of culture and history.

An individual acting out an invented life projects a magnetism that depends not at all on the virtue (or otherwise) of his cause. He lives a narrative that everyone affected by modern storytelling (from Conrad's novels to *The Bourne Ultimatum*) will recognize immediately as exciting and daring, no matter how perverse the motives for subterfuge.

The Mafia murderer whose confession got his bosses convicted, marooned in Omaha by the Witness Protection Program, and the brave detective who disguises himself as a biker to infiltrate the Hells Angels in Montreal, both live in the same furtive, eerie half-light, their existence endangered at every moment. So does the jihad warrior who waits in obscurity for the moment when he will be told to execute some monstrous crime. The renegade African dictator hiding in Riyadh at the capricious pleasure of the local princes and our own Igor Gouzenko, roosting in suburban Toronto under a false name for 37 years, fearing the rage of Stalin or his successors, have one thing in common: every moment of their lives must be lived in secret. They share in the mystery and the allure of elaborate, detailed mendacity. It is the ultimate in private life, every movement and word shrouded in fiction. The more or less ordinary secrets many people carry around (income-tax fiddles, adultery, stock fraud, etc.) are nothing beside the total secrecy of the underground man.

Generations ago the mobility of the modern age made self-reinvention a normal passage in many lives. Without it we would lack some of our most familiar characters, like the engineer whose ingenuity and energy lift him to billionaire status, or the street musician transformed into a star by a sudden hit. The underground man merely takes this same impulse of reinvention to a higher level, wiping clean his past as he endures a previously unimagined present and, often, a terrifying future. He's like many people who live among us, but much more so. His fascination rests partly on our sense that we will never know the truth of his story; at best our understanding of his life will depend on rumours. Even those few spies who describe their hidden lives feel constrained to convert their experience into fiction, as Somerset Maugham did in 1928 with his not quite credible book of stories, *Ashenden* (1927), or as le Carré did with his totally convincing series of books about George Smiley and his fellow agents in Britain.

Once in a long while someone who nursed a secret for decades reveals what he claims as the "truth"; usually it turns out to be a more extended version of the lies he lived by. The perfect example was *My Silent War*, the 1968 memoir of Kim Philby, most prominent of the Cambridge spies who began serving the Soviet Union in the 1930s. That book read as if edited (if not actually dictated) by the KGB, Philby's hosts in Moscow during his final decades. Neither he nor any of his colleagues has cared to tell us with precision or insight about the emotional experience of living a long career of prevarication. Not one of Gouzenko's eight children has so far given us an account of the family's life in hiding, though it could well be a valuable contribution to the literature of political stealth.

And, no matter how riveting it might be, it seems unlikely that we'll ever see such a document from the most successful secrets-keeper of modern times, the vile but amazingly resourceful Theodore Kaczynski, the Unabomber. A brilliant young mathematician, he turned against his profession and against most of humanity not long after earning his PhD. Holed up in a remote cabin in Montana, he decided that the best way to express his views about the ruin of the natural environment and the psychological manipulation of his fellow citizens was through a mail-bomb campaign that eventually killed three people and injured 23.

What has always seemed most remarkable about him was his ability to plot and execute his crimes without ever indicating, to even a single human being, that he was doing anything at all notable. Every criminal who depends on secrecy realizes that collaborators or confidants pose the greatest risk to success, but (so far as the record shows) no one, except Kaczynski, seems to have taken the obvious step of completely avoiding human contact. Try to imagine how he mentally sustained himself without a word of response from anyone.

His capacity for solitude seems to have been almost inhuman. Think of the phenomenal patience this maniac must have taught himself. From 1978 to 1995, he spoke to no one about what he was doing and carried out his atrocities without leaving a trace of a clue. He made the bombs himself, from commonplace and untraceable materials, then mailed them from many different places, each far from where he was living. It became obvious that he had chosen corporate executives and computer experts as his victims, but at some point he realized that his crimes were not making his ideological position clear. He could presumably have gone on killing forever, but instead felt the world had to know his thinking. At long last he was undone by what he must have believed would never touch him, a need for recognition.

In 1995 he wrote a letter to the *New York Times* promising to stop bombing provided the *Times* or the *Washington Post* published his manifesto, "Industrial Society and Its Future," denouncing the destruction of freedom by technology. When it appeared in print his brother recognized Kaczynski's style of argument and informed the FBI. On a guilty plea he received a life sentence with no possibility of parole. He's now over 75. In theory he could, if prison has calmed his mind, produce a valuable account of high intelligence turned perverse in total secrecy.

Archie Belaney, born in a small English town in 1888, practised a comparatively benign form of secrecy and deception. He was an unhappy child, abandoned by his father, but he nourished himself on

a dream of life among the Indians in Canada. When he arrived here
at the age of 17 he decided to become an Indian, at least partly. He
studied the wilderness with the Ojibwa in northern Ontario and slowly
concocted his legend. He invented appropriate details for anyone who
asked, as many did, once he became famous: he said he was born in
Hermosillo, Mexico, to Katherine Cochise, of the Apaches, and George
MacNeil, a Scot who served in the Indian wars as a scout and ended up
with his friend Buffalo Bill Cody's Wild West Show.

Grey Owl darkened his skin, braided his black hair, and on occasion
added a feather. He wore fringed buckskins and moccasins, with a
knife at his belt. He became the non-Indian's idea of an Indian. When
he began writing for publication, his literary style was as mannered
as his personality – fierce, stern, proud, a Noble Savage in the old
European sense. When his picture was taken he assumed a scowl that
he seems to have believed indicated the attitude of an Indian. In the
1930s his writings on the wilderness made him a hero of the conser-
vation movement. Touring England in 1937, he was so popular that he
was received by King George VI and the two princesses, Elizabeth and
her sister Margaret. He began his lecture with a few words in Ojibwa,
translating for the king: "I come in peace, brother."

In 1938, within days of his death, those who knew something of the
truth began talking about him, first of all to a correspondent from the
Toronto Star. It turned out that many of his acquaintances had suspect-
ed for years his story about an Indian mother. Some of them believed
he was a McGill graduate from a prosperous family in Montreal. When
his true history emerged, it turned out that there were several women
who were especially interested in what had become of him: "GREY OWL
HAD COCKNEY ACCENT AND FOUR WIVES," said one headline in Britain. *The Times* of London asked, "Who was he really, this mysterious
Grey Owl? The strange bird seems to be acquiring as many birthplaces
as Homer, as many wives as Solomon."

Canada has produced one other much-published faker, Frederick
Philip Grove, who began teaching school in small-town Manitoba in
1912 and soon started writing fiction, essays, and poetry. He was never
notably successful, but there were always publishers willing to issue
his books about rural life and critics willing to take him seriously. One

critic accurately said he was "acknowledged but unread – an author with a reputation and no public." Admittedly, his writing was clumsy, but it impressed some readers with its deep sincerity; he was admired for introducing realism to Canadian literature.

One work of fiction was his highly imaginative autobiography, *In Search of Myself*, which won a Governor General's Award for non-fiction in 1946. Careless inconsistencies in his story led to suspicions that he was less than truthful, but in his lifetime his official biography was never publicly challenged. When he died in 1948 at his last home in Simcoe, Ontario, his 18-year-son, Arthur, had no idea who he was or where he came from. Many years later, when I met him, Arthur was spending a great deal of time trying to uncover his father's origins.

In the end, a professor of English at Queen's University, D.O. Spettigue, after long research, came upon the name of a German author, Felix Paul Greve, who was in fact Grove in an earlier life. Spettigue's *FPG: The European Years*, published in 1973, outlined a dodgy history. In his native Germany Greve was fairly well known as a writer and translator but also as something of a crook. He spent months in prison for defrauding a friend and later managed to sell the rights to a major translation project to two separate publishers; that may have been why he seems to have faked his suicide before he abruptly departed from Germany for the United States in 1909.

Like many prolific authors, Greve/Grove left behind unpublished manuscripts, but they unfortunately contain no account of his adventures as two different people in two different countries. It would be interesting to know why he chose, for his legend, a new name that would eventually, under the pressure of scholarship, yield his secret. It would be even more interesting to know something about the emotional cost of living two such separate lives, and existing for so long within the contours of a lie that he himself had drawn.

But it is in the nature of such lives that we can know little more than an outline of the facts. Sophocles wrote that we should "Do nothing secretly; for Time sees and hears all things, and discloses all." Not really. Time sees and hears only a part of the truth. The rest must be left to the imagination.

TLS

THE TIMES LITERARY SUPPLEMENT

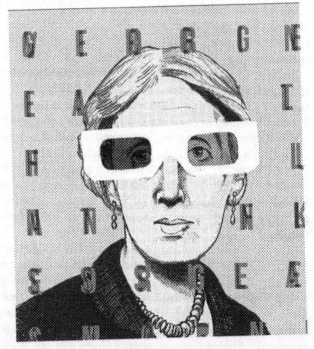

How to read

Looking at George Eliot through Virginia Woolf's eyes

Neither Times nor Literary nor Supplement

Long, long ago there was an overly chatty barber.
"How would you like me to cut your hair?" he asked.
"In silence," his customer replied.

This was considered a joke in ancient Rome, and it's the kind of item I cherish in my favourite periodical, the *Times Literary Supplement*. For more than a century the TLS has been spreading knowledge and wisdom across the world while simultaneously displaying for its readers an ever-expanding treasury of arcane knowledge.

No truth, no thought, is alien to the TLS. Its wings spread wide enough to encompass quantum physics and T.S. Eliot, ornithology and Bob Dylan, adultery and Machiavelli, public debt and Islamic architecture. It makes all of these subjects, and more, coherent to the non-expert and treats each of them in the appropriate tone, from dignified to derisory. I've read it for decades and can't imagine life without it. If they doubled the price tomorrow I'd obediently write them a larger cheque. Mario Vargas Llosa has been reading the TLS since he learned English 40 years ago: "It is the most serious, authoritative, witty, diverse and stimulating cultural publication in all the five languages I speak."

Roman humour, a subject few of us have ever explored, came to me on one of the blogs that TLS editors produce from time to time. Mary Beard, a classics professor at Cambridge and a TLS editor, wrote about the book she's finishing, *Laughter in Ancient Rome: On Joking, Tickling, and Cracking Up* (2014), which I will be anxious to read when the University of California Press publishes it in the summer.

Beard explains that the barber story appears in the *Philogelos*, a collection of more than 200 Roman jokes, though it's written in Greek. "Exactly the same gag," Beard tells us, is attributed by Plutarch to Archelaus, a Macedonian king in the fifth century BCE. Beard has also learned that in the twentieth century it was credited to Enoch Powell, the right-wing British MP, and to get the footnote right she's checked with a Powell expert.

In her blog she writes about her family, her love of beer, her gratitude to the editors of her books, and her travel, such as a recent visit to Rome

IN 2019 THE TLS ADOPTED ITS WIDELY-USED ACRONYM AS ITS PRIMARY NAMESAKE for the exhibition celebrating the 2,000th anniversary of the death of the Emperor Augustus. She's a don, but her tone is not donnish.

Readers who haven't recently looked at the TLS may be surprised to find that staff members write blogs. Regular subscribers know that in this way it's entirely up to date. It has created not only a version to be read on a smart phone but also an edition for tablets, where its excellent photographs look better than on the newsprint it has used since it began in 1902.

With persistence, talent, and a sense of purpose, a periodical creates its own unique environment, a structure where the subjects it deals with can flourish. Over time the publication begins to look something like a theatre company or an architectural firm, with its stars, its styles, and its delicately carved frame of reference. Eventually, if things work out, it becomes an essential institution. That's the case with the TLS.

But if a capacious sensibility is the paper's essential quality, that's not necessarily a source of pleasure to all of the readers. Some find it too much of a good thing. Some feel guilty about the many articles they ignore. Lydia Davis, the much-admired writer of short stories and translator of Proust, went so far as to declare her feelings in a quasi-poem, "How I Read as Quickly as Possible Through My Back Issues of the TLS" which she published in the January issue of Harper's and will include in her forthcoming book.

"I do not want to read about the life of Jerry Lewis," Davis wrote, beginning a list of what she refuses to read about: Mammalian carnivores, a portrait of a castrato, the history of the panda in China, a dictionary of women in Shakespeare, bumblebees, Ronald Reagan, The Oxford Companion to Canadian Military History. On the other hand she admitted to reading about the lectures of Borges, the social value of altruism, the building of the Pont Neuf, dust jackets in the history of bibliography, beer, East Prussia after World War II, philosemitism, and the Southport Lawnmower Museum. She thus revealed herself as an ideal TLS reader, since her list of inclusions is as extensive as the list of subjects she rejects. Still, I don't see how anyone can ignore a TLS article on bumblebees.

Those who try to define the category of this exceptional journal sometimes borrow a famous line from Voltaire ("the Holy Roman Empire was neither holy, nor Roman, nor an empire") and point out that the TLS is neither *Times* nor Literary nor Supplement. It's owned by the Murdoch corporation that controls the *Times* of London, but its appearance and content owe nothing to the daily newspaper. Nor is it literary, in any strict sense, since the pieces about literature are only a part of its content. When it began, however, it was in fact a supplement of the *Times*, and it contained mainly material about books. In 1914 it began to appear as a separate publication. Its range of subjects seems to have reflected a perception that literature can be seen best against an educated sense of society, politics, and the natural world.

For many decades it existed in an atmosphere of delicious mystery. Long after just about every other journal in English began publishing bylines, all TLS reviews appeared anonymously. I can remember the professional gossip this created. If England contained in 1960 two acknowledged experts on, say, Titian, and if one of them wrote a book about him, it was assumed by everyone that the subtly dismissive review was written by his rival. If a general's memoirs explained how he won the war, the review harshly contesting his claim was obviously written by a colleague who had despised him since Dunkirk. I remember being assured that "everyone" knew the truth, everyone being a few hundred people who had some connections with the editors.

Anonymity had its advantages. In the early days, editors with limited budgets were glad to hide the fact that a few reviewers were writing much of the paper. Bruce Richmond, the editor who created the TLS during 35 years on the job, made one notable discovery in the early days. Through family connections he met a bright 23-year-old, Virginia Stephen, later to be Virginia Woolf. From the start she was wondrously witty and perceptive, and Richmond used her as often as he could, up to 50 or 60 times a year. As she acknowledged, this was where she learned to write for the public.

Over the years of anonymity, piquant speculation only enhanced the question of an important review's authorship. All this changed in 1974, when an excellent new editor, John Gross, began introducing bylines. He thought that reviewers should take responsibility for their opinions.

I remember that Alfred Knopf, the dean of New York publishers, was appalled. He felt that anonymity had curbed the egotism of reviewers and kept the TLS honest. Perhaps, but it has been a much more interesting journal since reviewers' names began appearing.

For much of its life the TLS has had a reputation for intelligent, well-argued judgement. But those who know its history understand that its record was once considered spotty. During the first year a reviewer wondered whether Henry James' *The Wings of the Dove* (1902) was satisfactory "for short railway journeys and drowsy hammocks," and another couldn't see the point of Conrad's *Heart of Darkness* (1899). On Chekhov's death, two years later, the TLS suggested "he may or may not have been a man of genius."

Ulysses didn't even get mentioned at its first appearance in 1922 in Paris (it was banned in Britain); the 1936 English edition rated only a brief review. D.H. Lawrence's *The Rainbow* (1915) and Ford Madox Ford's *The Good Soldier* (1915) were ignored. Eliot's poetry was described as uninspired and "verging sometimes on the catalogue." (Eliot, a good sport, later became a frequent reviewer.) Another kind of classic, *The Wind in the Willows* (1908), was called "a book with hardly a smile in it."

The paper is edited with the greatest care, which makes its rare editorial disasters far more notable than they would be in a lesser publication. David Gallagher, writing from Chile in the letters column in December 2013, reported on a truly monstrous error (or instance of sabotage) that marred his recent piece on Mario Vargas Llosa. Gallagher wrote that Vargas Llosa has become "a passionate defender of liberal democracy." To Gallagher's astonishment, this was changed to a "passionate defender of the right-wing, neocon, authoritarian establishment." The TLS was apparently too traumatized to give a detailed explanation; it called this an error, apologized, and corrected it in the online version.

Over the years I've often noticed that the TLS editors are particularly adept at producing absorbing and valuable articles about books they don't particularly admire. This was the case with *Salinger* (2013), by David Shields and Shane Salerno, a huge and ugly 704-page monster that emerged from the depths of American journalism last fall. The TLS gave it two full pages by James Campbell, a specialist in American literature, who took this opportunity to think his way through J. D. Salinger's career rather than the book that occasioned his essay. He found the account of Salinger's life "impertinent in its rush to judgement on ... his human appetites and foibles, and even his single testicle, which offers David Shields licence to indulge in a characteristic bit of – well, bollocks."

Given that most TLS contributors are writers of some repute, they are not known for their egotism. Even so, there is one moment every year when a certain rivalry surfaces. It happens each November, when contributors are asked to name recent books they have admired. This results in eight or nine pages of what we might call competitive choosing, pages that devoted readers study with great intensity. Somehow, writers who are never condemned for showing off in their reviews are transformed into exhibitionists anxious to impress us with the originality, obscurity, or eccentricity of their selections.

Alex Danchev cites the sort of book we might expect in this feature, the *Notebooks of Albert Camus*, including a sample entry: "An intellectual is someone whose mind watches itself." But elsewhere the choices, as often as not, tend toward the obscure. Clare Griffiths names *Calon: A Journey to the Heart of Welsh Rugby* (2013), and Gabriel Josipovici suggests *The Lost Carving* (2012), about a year spent restoring the Hampton Court carvings of Grinling Gibbons, severely damaged by fire. Frederic Raphael expresses affection for a book about the American rowing team that surprised and humiliated Hitler by winning a gold medal at the 1936 Olympics. A.E. Stallings moves farther off the beaten track by recommending *Faces of Love* (2013), translations of three fourteenth-century Persian poets. George Steiner, the polyglot critic, normally wins this competition with critical books that originated in foreign languages. This winter he exceeded even his own standards by recommending Piero Boitani's magnificent survey of the role of the stars in human consciousness. Alas, the translation from the Italian hasn't yet been published, so for the time being we must rely, as we often do, on Steiner's account.

In that same survey Beverley Bie Brahic named Alice Munro's *Selected Stories*, adding that "Maybe only a Canadian who lives outside Canada can recognize the perfect pitch of Munro's tales." Ferdinand Mount, a former editor of the TLS, wrote: "Impossible to stifle a whoop of joy on hearing that Alice Munro had won the Nobel. No writer I know of gets at life the way she does." Reminding us that the TLS often gets it dead right.

Emperor Julian and
the Gods of Homer

19TH CENTURY ILLUSTRATION SHOWING EMPEROR JULIAN HELD ALOFT BY HIS TROOPS. PUBLIC DOMAIN

Counterfactual speculation, the detailed exploration of great events that never happened, can be one of the most agreeable ways to argue about the past. It licences us to think thoughts that are otherwise unthinkable and consider concepts that history has foreclosed. Winston Churchill wrote an essay about what might have happened if Robert E. Lee had won the Battle of Gettysburg. Niall Ferguson edited a delightful collection, *Virtual History: Alternatives and Counterfactuals* (1997), to consider such questions as what would have changed if there had been no American Revolution or if Germany had invaded Britain in May 1940.

My favourite high school teacher, a man born with the beautiful name of John Sage, sent me down this track in the middle of the last century by exhibiting great enthusiasm for the theory that if the Persian Empire instead of the Greek cities had won the Battle of Salamis in 480 BCE, Western civilization would never have got off the ground. We who listened to him had never heard of Salamis, barely knew Persia existed, and had at best a nodding acquaintance with Western civilization. Still, it sounded important, and I have never since thought of that battle without hearing John Sage's voice lovingly relating it.

Recently my own counterfactual imagination has turned toward the fate of Flavius Claudius Julianus Augustus, also known as Julian the Apostate, the Roman emperor for a brief moment, 361-363 CE. What if he had not died in battle but had instead remained on the throne for a dozen years or even longer? What if he had been given time to spread his favourite policy throughout the empire and arrange for a successor who was committed to his views?

Julian was born in Constantinople, a member of the Constantinian dynasty; his father was half-brother to Constantine the Great. Julian was raised as a Christian but learned from books the stories of the Greek gods. They attracted him by their energy, their imagination, and their innate comedy. By then, of course, they were officially dead. When Constantine converted the empire to Christianity, he declared all of them obsolete. The emerging Christian priests frowned on them and let their temples fall into disrepair unless they were suitable for converting into churches.

They were all to be forgotten – Mars and Venus, Apollo and Hermes, Diana and Neptune, the lot. But not by Julian. He became a covert polytheist. For years he attended Christian churches and carefully studied the Gospels, but in private his affections moved steadily toward the old gods. This would have been a purely personal issue if his family had not developed a habit of murdering its own members. Constantinian cousins, uncles, half-brothers, and others were done away with by their fellow Constantinians, in order to reduce the number of possible pretenders to the throne. Julian's predecessor, Constantius II, emperor from 337 to 361 CE, was the bloodiest of them. He purged almost the whole bloodline, till only Julian was left standing. He then promoted Julian to caesar, a kind of subordinate emperor, in charge of subduing Gaul under the supervision of the real emperor. Finally, Julian, with the enthusiastic backing of his troops, promoted himself to emperor.

That was when he revealed his plan – what followers of Canadian politics would call his hidden agenda. He wanted to turn back the clock of Christianization and reimpose pagan worship throughout the Roman Empire. No less than a whole civilization was at stake; he spoke of "the gods of Homer." It fell to him to save that entire world of wisdom and storytelling.

He did not propose to outlaw Christianity. He claimed Christians could remain Christians as Jews could remain Jews; he proposed even to rebuild the Second Temple in Jerusalem. (It is said Jewish opinion was ambivalent on this project.) Julian passed a rule guaranteeing that all religions were equal, which he saw as the Roman Empire's return to its original religious eclecticism.

But he refused to see the Hellenistic gods, his gods, dishonoured. In his eagerness, he moved rather too quickly. When he decided to resurrect an ancient oracular spring at a temple to Apollo near the Greek city of Antioch, he learned that the bones of a third-century martyred bishop now occupied the space. He ordered the bones taken elsewhere, which local Christians greeted with an enormous procession of protest. The temple then burned down, which Julian guessed (incorrectly, it turned out) was an act of Christian vengeance.

He began sacrificing various animals to his gods and was in some circles nicknamed "bull-burner." Christians put it about that in his zeal to propitiate the inhabitants of Mount Olympus he sacrificed a woman, a nasty rumour his friends were quick to deny.

He portrayed himself as tolerant of Christians, but he found them a pest. He refused even to call them Christians, which he saw as a recognition that Jesus was divine; instead he called them Galileans, after Galilee, the place where Jesus spent most of his life.

Julian hated the bitter, boring doctrinal disputes of the bishops. He wrote at one point that under his predecessor Christians were allowed to exile, imprison, and sometimes massacre each other for heresy. When he became emperor he called home the alleged heretics (including some dissident bishops), liberated those who were imprisoned on grounds of doctrine and, as he put it, "compelled" the Christians to live in peace.

So far as he could tell the Christians did not appreciate his generosity: "Such is the restless rage of these Galileans that they deplore their inability any longer to devour one another."

That forceful irony was typical of his writing. Among rulers he was highly educated. He hoped some day to be recognized as a philosopher; he often consulted philosophers, and he wrote out of a confident understanding of the Neoplatonic philosophy developed in the previous two centuries. His style is one reason he received an enthusiastic review from Edward Gibbon in one of the great monuments of European culture, *The History of the Decline and Fall of the Roman Empire* (1776).

Gibbon was not renowned for his love of the old gods, but he was certainly no admirer of early Christianity; he shared Julian's view that the Christians were a baleful influence.

Julian was brought up in a kind of royal prison. He lived in sumptuous surroundings and had every advantage but freedom. His life was supervised by tutors and spies selected by the emperor; he was told where to live and where he might occasionally travel. The emperor's paranoia focused on the possibility of a coup organized around Julian.

All this makes it especially remarkable that he developed into an

intellectual, eager to develop his own ideas. He was flexible enough
to study war as an academic subject and then become, during his
first whiff of battle, a talented general. Because the exact year of his
birth remains obscure we don't know how long it took him to live all
these lives. But he was either 31 or 32 when he died.

An emperor who had dreamt of a new beginning for the gods
turned out to be the last pagan, a curtain falling on the drama of
Olympus. An apocryphal story had Julian, on his deathbed, speaking
to Jesus: "You have won, Galilean." This was later shown to have been
invented long after he died, but as a story it survived at least until
1866, when Algernon Swinburne inserted it in his "Hymn to Proser-
pine": "Thou hast conquered, O pale Galilean; the world has grown
grey from thy breath ..."

Today the ancient gods linger in our language – words like
"mercurial," "titanic," "fortune," "martial," and "psychological" are
distant reminders of the deities Julian wanted to preserve. In the
museums they appear far less often than biblical figures, but they
do appear – in fact it was the study of Bernini's magnificent baroque
images of antique gods at the Galleria Borghese in Rome that recently renewed my interest in Julian and his arguments.

The Julian Society (juliansociety.org), headquartered in Maine,
pursues its goal of presenting its hero's life as an example of "pagan
piety, dignity, respectability and social responsibility" – the very
phrase "pagan piety" seems to come from another world, so accustomed are we to think of pagans as outside the realm of sanctity.

The society puts up a brave front, announcing proudly its slogan:
"As long as one person worships truly, the ancient Gods and Goddess-
es are with us." It carries news, for instance, of a recent meeting to
discuss the esoteric Mithras, the Sun God, whose priests (it is said)
conducted Julian through the mysteries of the Mithraic cult and
made him an initiate, in his view one of the great events of his life.

While the dreams of the Julian Society are unlikely to be fulfilled,
the last 300 years have been better for Julian's reputation than the
previous millennium. For centuries after his death the Christians
owned his name as they owned civilized discourse across Europe.
"Julian" was a synonym for betrayal, or even sin. But whenever

Christianity has been questioned, Julian has received his due, or some part of it.

In the sixteenth century Michel de Montaigne, the first great essayist, declared that Julian as a philosopher king could be compared to Alexander the Great. In the 1680s in England Julian was recruited by enemies of the Roman Catholics who deployed him as an early version of Protestantism, a noble critic of popery.

It was Voltaire, however, who became Julian's greatest champion by emphasizing his tolerance. In *The Philosophical Dictionary* Voltaire argued that after 1,400 years it was time for enlightened men to revise the judgment on Julian. The record shows him to be "sober, chaste, disinterested and brave"; but because he was not a Christian, "he has long been considered a monster."

Voltaire believed Julian had all the qualities of Trajan, with the exception of his depraved taste; all the virtues of Cato, without his obstinacy or ill-humour; everything good about Julius Caesar and none of his vices. "He was in all respects equal to Marcus Aurelius, who was reputed the first of men."

Julian has since received no equal encomium, but neither has anyone else. He's remained interesting mainly to a minority. In 1870 Henrik Ibsen wrote an enormously ambitious play, *Emperor and Galilean*, which begins with Julian's youth and his attraction to the gods. It ends with his death in Mesopotamia at the hands of a Christian fanatic hell-bent on martyrdom. Ibsen wrote it in ten acts, which on stage would last perhaps nine hours.

It was performed in Oslo and Leipzig in Ibsen's lifetime, then abandoned to the libraries. Finally, in 2011, the National Theatre in London gave the play its first English-language production, 105 years after Ibsen's death. The script by Ben Power eliminated many characters and cut the play to a manageable, well-reviewed three hours. Jonathan Kent, the director, stressed the point behind the production: Julian stood at a crossroad in history as the spiritual future of the West was being defined.

A more recent work of the creative imagination, Gore Vidal's 1964 historical novel *Julian*, provides a hint of where we would be now if Julian had not been denied his wishes. Vidal tells a highly readable story through an autobiography that Julian is said to have written late in his life. We meet a rather lovable man, curious and articulate, who in his private moments reveals himself as self-reflective, self-doubting, self-critical, sometimes self-pitying, as modern as Hamlet.

Our world would probably have done to the old gods what Vidal does to Julian: we would have made them more like ourselves, as we try to do with Jesus, Moses, and every other figure in the Bible. If the age of secularism developed as it in fact has done, we might well treat Greek deities as we treat those who originated in the Middle East. On Sunday mornings in 2011 there would be many more temples we would not go to, and many more gods in whom we would not believe. But the courses in comparative religion would be vastly more amusing.

Nostalgia and the
Lies of the Past

GARGOYLE, NOTRE DAME CATHEDRAL, PARIS. GETTY IMAGES

Like cars or buildings or computers, the images that shape the ways we see the world inevitably deteriorate and lose value. Spiritual entropy erodes them. To quote Neil Young quoting an ad of long ago, rust never sleeps. When an image stands for a nation, or a national tradition, it requires frequent attention. From time to time it must be revived, a process that may require dubious cultural strategies.

One day in 1953, 21 years old, seeing Paris for the first time, I climbed 380 steps to the balustrade of Notre Dame Cathedral. There I took a photograph that managed to be both appallingly hackneyed and historically misguided. It has since been lost, fortunately, but I remember that it showed a gargoyle gazing over the rooftops of Paris.

Within the next day or two it became obvious to me that the image I had chosen was a ubiquitous cliché in a city long notorious for visual clichés. Everywhere I went, bookstore or flea market or restaurant, I came upon the same gargoyle-surveys-Paris conceit, usually better composed but otherwise close to identical. People bad been coming up with that idea for generations, obviously. Some photographers had even used precisely the same gargoyle, the pensive horned demon of the north tower, lost in thought, head in hands as he confronts the world – "my gargoyle," as I had imagined. Not for the last time, I had in my small way played youth's most familiar role, re-inventing the wheel.

Years later it also became clear that my picture was taken under a false impression, the assumption (still shared by most visitors, apparently) that those gargoyles, being attached to a thirteenth-century Gothic cathedral, are therefore thirteenth-century gargoyles, give or take a century. Reason suggests that their grotesque faces represent some version of Gothic evil or comedy or both. This could result in many interesting generalizations, all of them baseless. As I eventually learned, the 54 stone creatures on the balustrade were designed and produced in the middle of the nineteenth century; they are the contemporaries not of the medieval architects but of the engineers who developed the steamship, the spinning jenny, and other landmark inventions of the industrial revolution. They are, in short, modern.

Installed in millions of imaginations by generations of photographers, they distribute a pervasive falsehood, the perfect stone embodiment of Voltaire's remark that history consists of lies on which we agree. They represent the often questionable role of nostalgia in our encounter with half-understood ancient buildings.

These icons are the result of ingeniously manufactured nostalgia, part of the elaborate fraud famously unveiled by E. J. Hobsbawm in 1983 when he edited *The Invention of Tradition*. Hobsbawm and his colleagues pointed out that many practices and rituals believed to be deeply traditional were invented in recent centuries. Most of the ceremonies by which Elizabeth II was ritually crowned monarch had been devised since 1870, for instance. (I was one of her majesty's subjects who watched her crowned on new TV sets in 1952, in the certain conviction that the solemn anointing of her breast and other rituals came down to us from our ancient past.) In the same book Hugh Trevor-Roper wrote that the Scottish Highland tradition was a modern invention, that the kilt was invented by an Englishman in 1730, and that "clan tartans" were devised in the nineteenth century.

In Japan in 1997 I went to a rural restaurant, Ukai Toriyama, where guests cook their food over charcoal braziers in little huts surrounded by carp ponds. Elegant, kimono-clad waitresses bustle about, every gesture a ceremony, delivering vegetables, fish, and meat. Torches blaze on the paths in the surrounding forest. Time stops. Every detail reflects centuries of tradition – or so it seemed. But in truth, this kind of restaurant was invented only a few years earlier, not only to please foreigners like me but, even more, to affirm *nihonjinron*, Japanese uniqueness. The Japanese (as much as the English inventing a fictional royal ceremony) search endlessly for their authentic selves. It is a question of "sacralizing" the present, as cultural theorists say, injecting meaning into contemporary existence by borrowing eloquent fragments of the past.

In an image reproduced in February by the *New York Times*, Frank Lloyd Wright, wearing his familiar white suit and hat, leans against one of several redwood trees that have emerged inside his most famous building, the Guggenheim Museum in New York. The artwork, *FLW in His Element*, shows cracks in the building, birds flying across his famous space, and plants spilling over the edges of the open floors behind him. We are looking at the results of an apocalypse or at a time after New York has been abandoned by its residents and returned to nature. But Wright, in spirit, remains standing. The digital print appears in an exhibition, *Contemplating the Void: Interventions in the Guggenheim Museum*, celebrating the building's fiftieth anniversary. Saunders Architecture, a firm in Norway, sent this work as a tribute to Wright's stature, his relationship with nature, and the longevity of Wright's most famous space.

At this difficult moment in history, the Guggenheim functions as the perfect American icon. In retrospect, that seems to have been its main function from the beginning. Certainly it doesn't work as a place to display paintings. I admired it the week it opened, when a collection from the museum's warehouse filled the walls; you could stand in one place and survey the whole gallery at once, picking out favourite paintings here and there, enjoying it as if it were an art book with all the pages open at once. But a few weeks later, back there to see a show I wanted to study in detail, a survey of Wassily Kandinsky's career, I discovered that in this art museum it was impossible to see the art. No matter where you stood, someone always walked in front of you. Being on a slanting floor soon lost its novelty value and turned into a serious distraction.

Even so, the building retains a potent message. In the unique grammar of Wright, the most American of Americans, it speaks the language of individualism. In a city that in 1959 was mainly committed to a sterile modernism, Wright's Guggenheim expressed itself through a contrarian collection of gentle curves and a shell-like rotunda that seems borrowed from the sea. Few buildings of modern times carry such bracing emotion.

This winter and spring the Los Angeles County Museum of Art has been showing *American Stories: Paintings of Everyday Life, 1765-1915*. Borrowed from the Metropolitan in New York, it sets out to redefine America by considering its history through the iconic pictures produced by great painters, among them Mary Cassatt, Thomas Eakins, Winslow Homer, and John Singer Sargent. The reviewer for the *Los Angeles Times*, Christopher Knight, took an elegiac tone: "What is an American?" he asked. The receding of the "American Century" and "the national nervous breakdown unleashed by the 9/11 terrorist attacks" had put national identity in question. *American Stories* seems "prompted by this deep unease."

The exhibition turns to history – and nostalgia. It grounds itself in an era when America (at least in memories coloured by intense nostalgia) was not only young and vital but confident and uncomplicated. It attempts to ease the soul of this difficult time with classics like John Singleton Copley's depiction of Paul Revere, silversmith and Revolutionary War hero, holding his chin in his right hand and a silver teapot in his left; the teapot refers to the British tax on tea that helped set off the Revolution. As Knight says, "Copley's brilliant image fuses head and hand as tools for thought, labor and moral action. The portrait describes a person, but it places him in the context of an epic story."

Copley's pictures stand on their own as art, whether or not they are pressed into national service. But the same tendency loses its purchase on reality when Norman Rockwell, a celebrated magazine illustrator, becomes a national monument. At the Ringling Museum in Sarasota, Florida, this winter, the strain was beginning to show. "It would be almost anti-American for Norman Rockwell's work to be criticized, no matter how subtle the critique," said a quotation printed in the catalogue for *In Search of Norman Rockwell's America*. Furthermore, "Rockwell's work has become a symbol of all that's good in America." Those were the words of Ed Asner, the TV actor. Valerie Harper, another actor, said in the catalogue that Rockwell defined America: "He revealed how we were, how we still are, how we'll always be." And President Jimmy Carter suggested that "His work often shows the very best of American values and captures the quintessential American spirit that lives in each of us."

That exhibition, like many of the celebrations of Rockwell's art since his death in 1978, left the impression that Americans are less interested in enjoying him as an artist than in clinging to him as a moral life raft. The show at Ringling described itself as "groundbreaking" because a photographer named Kevin Rivoli took a series of photographs as parallels to the settings and models in Rockwell's illustrations and *Saturday Evening Post* covers – a bug-eyed soldier on kitchen duty reading the 1942 news from home; teenagers on a date; three baseball umpires making dismayed faces at the sky as rain begins falling; a gang of neighbours gathered to welcome a soldier home from the war in 1945.

Intended as a tribute to Rockwell and a way of enhancing the audience's idea of the material, Rivoli's photos instead subvert Rockwell's drawings, making them look even sillier and goofier than they would appear on their own. The photographs carry a sharp and often touching realism; the Rockwell characters, on the other hand, read like halfhearted caricatures.

Rockwell's admirers do him no favour by exhibiting him in museums as a brilliant chronicler of modern American culture. His art reduces the emotional power of whatever it touches, transforming American folklore into a series of sentimental parables and sour gags.

In the middle of the nineteenth century Notre Dame was crumbling, approaching the status of a ruin. It was most famous for Victor Hugo's 1831 novel about Quasimodo, the hunchback. Perhaps that book had drawn so much attention that King Louis-Philippe felt the cathedral deserved restoration. Perhaps a king ruling in a post-revolutionary age felt affectionate about a great monument representing a time when revolution was hardly imaginable. So France spent a sizable fortune on the four-decade project of bringing Notre Dame back to life. Eugène Viollet-le-Duc, the principal architect, had firm ideas about how it should be done: "To restore an edifice is not to maintain it, repair it or remake it, it is to re-establish it in a complete state that may never have existed at a given moment." He made Notre Dame into what he thought it should be, not what it had been. Reverence for the past surrendered to the ego of the architect and the pride of a nation that would soon be seeing itself as the centre of the modern world.

Viollet-le-Duc commissioned new windows, new paintings, and major architectural changes. Most of the sculptures that were once positioned on the balustrade had long since fallen to the ground, reduced to lumps of stone lying in the grass of the cathedral grounds. Viollet-le-Duc and his principal sculptor, Victor Planet, were free to re-imagine the sculptures to please themselves and their contemporaries.

Gothic sculpture had usually shown humans and human-like figures in groups, typically in clusters of roughly identical angels framing majestic doorways. That approach was of no interest to Viollet-le-Duc and Planet. As the late Michael Camille argued in his excellent history, *The Gargoyles of Notre-Dame* (2009), the new sculpture going up on the balustrade shifted the tone of the cathedral from Gothic to modern.

The nineteenth century was a boom time for sculptors. Every square in France exhibited sculptures conceived as tributes, what Camille calls "human egos made of stone." That bloated individualism became the style of the gargoyles. "This is what makes them so profoundly unmedieval," as Camille put it. That's why they impressed me even as they fooled me.

While imagining that I was confronting the sensibility of medieval Europe, the parent civilization of the modern West, I was attracted in a more commonplace way, by nimble variations on the civilization in which I had grown up. The Notre Dame gargoyles reflect the same cultural tone as fairy tales.

Each of them was "an egotistical, wilful beast driven by its own desire." They became, as Camille says, emblems of tormented human consciousness. That's the reason for the popularity of those images in the bookstores and elsewhere. Melancholy and isolated, the gargoyles attracted modern empathy. "People sensed a spark of something alive, a spirit, in the more animated eyes of demonic beasts." And up there at the top of Notre Dame, the great age of nostalgia was born, twisted and ironically misguided but nevertheless a great blessing to the tourist trade.

The Munro Woman: History as We Read It in the Stories of a Nobel Laureate

Robin lived just thirty miles from Stratford, Ontario, but she had never heard of anybody from her town going to see one of the Shakespeare plays. It was not something they did. It was beyond the circumference of their imagination. Robin's neighbour, Willard, was afraid of being looked down on by the other people in the audience, and afraid he wouldn't be able to follow the language. Joanne, Robin's older sister, was sure that no one, ever, really liked Shakespeare. If anybody from their town went to one of the plays it would be because they wanted to mix with the higher-ups who were not enjoying it themselves but were only letting on they were.

These characters appear in "Tricks" a story Alice Munro included in *Runaway*, her 2004 collection. It's a highly audacious story and unusual for Munro in its self-consciously literary quality.

The resolution turns on twins and mistaken identity, tricks often put to use by Shakespeare in *Twelfth Night* and elsewhere – which is one reason the Shakespeare festival plays a role. There's a chance meeting that seems likely to change lives, an outlandish coincidence and an obscure document, discovered a lifetime later, that reveals everything. Munro even points us toward the source of her trickery, in the way that Nabokov might.

Robin decides to try Stratford and Shakespeare, and for a while she attends one production a year, always a Saturday matinee, when the lowest ticket prices are available. While she knows no one who would want to discuss the play with her, it becomes a significant part of her inner life. It's a source of optimism: "Those few hours filled her with an assurance that the life she was going back to, which seemed so makeshift and unsatisfactory, was only temporary and could easily be put up with." Robin is so delicately and completely rendered, so obviously loved by her creator, that as I read "Tricks" for the third time, I felt an almost physical need to know that her yearning for happiness was realized. No such luck, but instead I marvelled at Munro's unrivalled ability to lay before us the mysterious unexpectedness of life.

"Tricks" is an uncommon example of Munro's writing, but at the core of it we find a familiar (and in my own opinion welcome)

ALICE MUNRO, 1982. PHOTO BY FRANZ MAIER FOR THE GLOBE AND MAIL.

Munro type. Robin exemplifies what I've come to think of as the Munro Woman, just as her sister, Joanne, plays with great accuracy the role of someone too ignorant to know anything but what she hates. The Munro Woman, in various guises, appears in stories throughout Munro's work, but she dominates *Runaway*. We usually meet her in the 1960s or 1970s, but sometimes Munro and her readers visit her many years later, to find out how her story turned out.

When encountered in adolescence the Munro Woman is typically a clever student who is doing her best to hide her cleverness. She's also more isolated than people like to be during adolescence, when they need friends to help them fight their parents. In high school she's lucky if she finds one or two girls who share her affliction of cleverness. I imagine many a female reader of Munro has sat up in excitement at a passage like: "In the town where she grew up her sort of intelligence was often put in the same category as a limp or an extra thumb, and people had been quick to point out the expected accompanying drawbacks ..." The community judges that a person so endowed will have a hard time in life and may never find a husband.

The Munro Woman may be articulate, but if she reveals her thoughts people say behind her back, "Your little friend is quite the intellectual, isn't she?" In another story the girl's father is desperately anxious that she learn to fit in. "You have to fit in, he told her, otherwise people will make your life hell."

Munro stories often take place in a world of jellied salads and cribbage players. In another story we encounter a parent with a remarkable prejudice: "Father has never taken to playing Bridge because he somehow thinks it's too High-Hat." These are people who know their place. They expect everyone around them, including members of their families, to absorb the same knowledge. The world Munro creates is ruled by a meticulously calibrated class system.

When Munro was young the first writers who really moved her were from the American South – Eudora Welty, Flannery O'Connor, Katherine Anne Porter, Carson McCullers. They were classed as "regional" writers, until critics finally realized that most of the good writing in the world is in some sense regional. Reading the southerners, Munro realized that she could write about small towns, rural people, and the life she knew well. She also noticed that women seemed capable of writing about the freakish, the marginal. That apparently made her comfortable. "I don't know how I got that feeling of being on the margins," she told a *Paris Review* interviewer. "Maybe it was because I grew up on a margin."

An element of autobiography goes into the making of the Munro Woman. Looking back on her youth, Munro once said, "I was brought up to believe that the worst thing you could do was 'call attention to yourself' or 'think you were smart.'" In the chronically unsmart, a hint of smartness brings out the nastiness.

Struggling against the claustrophobia of small-town life, her characters yearn for something better. Still, their hopes for the future are inchoate during adolescence and even later. They imagine there is a better life somewhere, and they nourish dreams of escape. They see no way to realize those dreams, and in the meantime they try as much as possible to act like everyone else.

Juliet, the central figure in three of the *Runaway* stories, has a talent and a love for classical literature. Her professors are delighted with her. "They were grateful these days for anybody who took up ancient languages." But they worry about her. "The problem was that she was a girl."

She was scholarship material, but if she married, they assumed, she would have wasted all her hard work and theirs. If she didn't marry she would probably lose out on promotions to men, who needed the good jobs to support families. "And she would not be able to defend the oddity of her choice of Classics, to accept what people would see as its irrelevance, or dreariness, ... Odd choices were simply easier for men, most of who would find women glad to marry them. Not so the other way around."

Even if they marry, their cleverness makes them look odd. In the story "Oranges and Apples" we encounter a married woman who spends much of her time reading authors such as Marcel Proust and Thomas Mann. Her mother-in-law can't condemn her for her taste but finds another way to point out her peculiarity and even brand her as reckless: "Barbara has a real mania for reading – isn't she worried about bringing all those books from the library into the house?

You never know who has been reading them."

Hazel, in "Hold Me Fast, Don't Let Me Pass," marries, at 18, a man who ends up working for his whole life in a friend's appliance store. Hazel is "shy, prudish, and intelligent. Jack triumphed easily over the shyness and prudery, and he was not as irritated as most men were, then, by the intelligence. He took it as a kind of joke." Of course he did.

How can these characters break from the pattern of their lives and escape the future that their communities and their families have defined for them? Often they decide to do something brave, original, and perhaps foolish by going off with the wrong man or at the last minute refusing the right man. Juliet travels a long distance to visit a man she has met briefly on a train, though he doesn't even know her last name. Another character, having come to believe that romance should involve passion, destroys her most obvious chance of marriage by going off for one wild night with the reckless, glamorous half-brother of the man she was expected to marry.

Their contemporaries look on these clever girls and women with fear – their intelligence seems dangerous, offensive, or at best tiresome. Women like this are trapped, but by what? By prejudice against women, to be sure, but also by a society that's determined to avoid any thought that appears difficult. Above all, they are trapped by their moment in history.

In 2004 Jonathan Franzen, writing in the *New York Times*, remarked that Munro wasn't as well appreciated as she should be. The reason, he said, is that she doesn't load onto her writing obvious themes. When you're reading Munro, you're "failing to multitask by absorbing civics lessons or historical data. Her subject is people. People people people."

That seems to me a colossal case of missing the point. It's true that Munro doesn't throw in great chunks of research (she never condescends to her readers). But the great unspoken theme of her work is history, the history of private life in her time and place, which also stands for many other places of the last five or so decades. Her work speaks of her era, to which she gives brilliant and perceptive shape.

Those who have lived through recent times can't fail to recognize, with either pain or delight or a combination of both, the characteristic ambition, ignorance, and yearning of this era. The way we treat each other, and the way we treated each other in the recent past, are woven into stories to powerful effect but without unnecessary explanation. Her subject in the beginning was her generation, but as she matured she broadened her scope to bring in a steadily wider field of vision.

Many real-life versions of the Munro Woman have existed in every corner of society, with all their resentments and hopes, all their unused talent and their derided intelligence, providing more material and more ways for Munro's imagination to express itself. They have been a gift to her talent, and she has given them in return a portrait of themselves.

Through the 1950s and the 1960s in North America a new generation of women was emerging, more or less in silence, waiting to articulate itself, hardly guessing that before the twentieth century ended the roles of the sexes in public and private would fundamentally change. In the last fifty or so years nothing more important than this evolution has happened in the democracies of the West; and no one has written about it with more subtlety and more acute observation than Munro. In 2013 the Nobel Prize for literature went to a master storyteller who also happened to be one of the great historians of her time.

24.

The Harsh Judgment
of the Museum

VENUS DE MEDICI, UFFIZI GALLERY, FLORENCE

Nathaniel Hawthorne was not at all pleased with the British Museum. Whatever charm it might have had was lost on him. One day in 1856 he wrote in his notebook that he found it exceedingly tiresome. "It quite crushes a person to see so much at once." Disheartened, he wandered from room to room. He found himself wishing ("Heaven forgive me!") that the frieze of the Parthenon, obtained by Lord Elgin from the Ottoman rulers in Athens, could be burnt into lime and the granite Egyptian statues cut into building stones. It occurred to him that it would be better if relics of ancient times disappeared with the generations that produced them. "The present is burthened too much with the past."

Is there even one museum visitor who has never, even for a moment, shared Hawthorne's feelings? Appointed US consul in Liverpool by President Franklin Pierce, he had many opportunities to study in detail the European culture that had always absorbed his attention. Yet on this occasion he was ungrateful for his opportunity. The reason is familiar. Like so many of us, he was afflicted by museum fatigue, the ailment that produces aching feet, tired legs, a sour disposition, and a desperate urge to escape. As William Empson wrote several generations later in his poem, "Homage to the British Museum," "People are continually asking one the way out." Are they seeking to leave because they are physically tired? Or is there a form of psychological unease lying beneath their discomfort?

Hawthorne, as it turned out, spent at least one happy day in a museum. He moved with his family to Italy in 1858 and stayed in a villa in Florence. There, in the octagonal gallery of the Uffizi Gallery where we can still see it, he encountered a Roman copy of a Greek sculpture, the *Venus de Medici*. He had heard so much about it that he felt his breath rise and fall as he walked toward it. He was not disappointed. It appealed to his erotic and sentimental instincts.

As his notebook says, "She is very beautiful, very satisfactory; and has a fresh and new charm.... I felt a kind of tenderness for her; an affection, not as if she were one woman, but all womanhood in one." He decided her modesty (she poses with one arm covering her breasts, the other reaching down to shield her vulva) "unmakes her as the heathen goddess, and softens her into woman.... I am glad to have seen this Venus, and to have found her so tender and so chaste."

He added an afterthought: "*The Venus de Medici* has a dimple in her chin."

It happens that I love the marble Venus he so admired and also love the plunging, snorting Athenian horses Lord Elgin brought home. Even though we differ on the second point, my heart goes out to Hawthorne. I have had some of the most exalting experiences of my life in museums – and some of the most miserable. Museums are designed as places of celebration and veneration, and almost every one of them will introduce us, if we allow it, to some enchanting and valuable aspect of civilization that we might otherwise miss. And yet a museum can be as lonely and alienating as any corner of the planet. Even as it parades incomparable riches before us it also creates, on certain occasions, a withering desolation of the spirit – a desolation so extreme that Hawthorne, a writer with a strong sense of history, found himself idly dreaming of a better world that casually abandoned physical evidence of the past.

Museums offer us "fact condensed in vivid imagery," as the critic Lawrence Alloway put it. By choosing objects that represent history at its greatest moments, they concentrate and crystallize an era or a school of art, giving it persuasive shape, taking powerful images from the places for which they were intended and relocating them within a context of scholarship modified by entertainment. They provide not "art" exactly, nor "history," but an intensified and specialized account of both.

Hawthorne lived in the first great age of museums. We live in the second. The nineteenth century created public institutions where the public could see the art accumulated by the rich and the noble as well as by adventurers and missionaries who brought back exotic art from across the globe. The central purpose of European museums, aside from satisfying the pride of those who donated art, was the moral betterment of the populace. They were gracious gestures made by the powerful to benefit the lowly.

Museums today have a radically different role. They serve the needs of the tourist industry, but they stand above all as emblems proclaiming the intelligence and ambition of the cities and nations that build them. According to Glenn Lowry, formerly the Art Gallery of Ontario director and now the head of the Museum of Modern Art in New York, "Every major city either wants an art museum or wants a bigger or better one." In Toronto the Royal Ontario Museum has redesigned itself architecturally, and in 2008 the Art Gallery of Ontario opened its transformed building. These are among scores of large-scale museum projects around the world early in the twenty-first century.

When Abu Dhabi decided that its new development on Saadiyat Island should begin life as a place with cultural status, it didn't try to create a great orchestra or a distinguished library. It signed a 30-year agreement with the Louvre to run Louvre Abu Dhabi, a $1.5 billion project. In authority, fame, and social status, museums have overtaken all other cultural institutions, including several that have a longer history: libraries, cathedrals, theatres, opera houses, even universities. More than any other physical structures, museums symbolize civilized accomplishment.

Planners and directors labour passionately to make them popular and beloved as well as respected. Nevertheless, there's something about a good museum that generates anxiety, the likely source of museum fatigue. And the greater the museum, the greater the possibility for anxiety.

In the summer of 1938 W.H. Auden wrote to a friend from Brussels: "I have been doing the art gallery and trying to appreciate Rubens. The daring and vitality take one's breath away, but what is it all ABOUT?"

Anyone familiar with Auden's magisterial attitude to culture will find it absurd that at age 31 he was still "trying to appreciate" any aspect of art, like some provincial culture vulture. That alone emphasizes the stern authority of a well-stocked museum. Auden seems never to have satisfied himself about the meaning of Rubens, but another work in the same building, Pieter Brueghel's *Landscape with the Fall of Icarus*, so stirred his sympathy that it inspired one of his most famous poems, "Musée des Beaux Arts." It was a painting clearly ABOUT something – suffering, and humanity's ability to ignore it.

"About suffering they were never wrong,/The old Masters," Auden began. He outlined Brueghel's scene: Icarus has flown too close to the sun on his wax wings, the sun has melted the wax, and he has fallen into the sea. All we see of him in the painting is a pair of legs vanishing into the Aegean. The myth usually serves as a warning against arrogance, but Auden (with Brueghel) focuses elsewhere: the landscape contains a fisherman, a shepherd, and a farmer who either fail to see Icarus's fall or don't care about it. A ship, glimpsed sailing past Icarus's legs, continues sailing. The workers have to keep working; the ship must travel on, and no one has time for anyone else's sudden death.

While Auden, who had recently rediscovered Christianity, looked for kindness and the recognition of a tragedy, he understood ruefully that "everything turns away" from individual sorrow. He sees (again with Brueghel) that no one should have to suffer alone while the world ignores his suffering; nevertheless, this is the human condition, compressed onto one canvas.

Auden's experience in Brussels doesn't demonstrate that Rubens is pointless and Brueghel engaging, though a thought like that may have passed through Auden's mind. For those who love museums it illustrates instead that we are always at the mercy of the protocols and expectations of museology. Learning them may be one of the few ways to evade (if only sometimes) "museum fatigue."

We routinely place art objects that are new to us in a perceptual realm that we have prepared – a grid of remembered images that constitute our visual knowledge. Museums decide, after generations of study and discussion, which objects to show us and how to place them within history and society. Each museumgoer, confronting the collection curators have arranged, must reconcile his or her private template with what the collection offers. The paintings of Rubens are ABOUT many things, but perhaps not things that corresponded with Auden's personal grid.

But we should never expect, or even hope, that a museum's organized collection will comfortably fit within our own system of taste, whatever that happens to be. Surprise should be part of exploring any collection. This is one way curators at their best serve as educators: they rattle our assumptions by disclosing the images and memories that make sense of our lives. They can help us understand why we think as we do. Why go to museums, asks Durs Grünbein, the contemporary German poet. Because "There you can see without interference how the battles of memory were fought. Where else could I, in the briefest amount of time, learn more about the way my brain works?"

But if it catches us at our most self-conscious, or confronts us with our guard down, a museum has the ability to judge us, perhaps harshly. On certain occasions it may find us guilty of ignorance or insensitivity. This may be why many people avoid museums entirely.

Perhaps the most eloquent account of museum-anxiety appears in Jean Stafford's autobiographical story, "Children Are Bored on Sunday," first published in the *New Yorker* in 1948. Stafford was a wonderfully talented writer who somehow placed herself in situations almost certain to provoke alcoholism, depression, and worse.

Her first husband was the poet Robert Lowell, famous as a serious drunk and a frequent resident of mental hospitals. Through him she met "the New York intellectuals," among whom she felt permanently a stranger – "a rube," as her character Emma defines herself. Stafford came from a modest family in the West and graduated from the University of Colorado. She found herself caught in a world where being an intellectual was a proud calling and Colorado was distant enough to be provincial but not distant enough to be exotic.

In the story Emma, like her creator, has been hospitalized for depression and alcoholism. On a Sunday afternoon she's spending time at the Metropolitan Museum when she sees Alfred Eisenburg, an intellectual with an "El Greco face," who has always made her feel an outsider. She's flirted with him, but he's one of the people she both envies and despises. (Eisenburg was based on Delmore Schwartz, a star of the *Partisan Review* crowd who eventually succumbed to depression, alcoholism, and paranoid schizophrenia. His friend Saul Bellow put his collapse at the centre of a much-admired novel, *Humboldt's Gift* (1975).

In self-reflection Emma slides from reminders of social humiliation to an ironic view of her flaws: "Her pretensions needed brushing; her ambiguities needed to be cleaned; her evasions would have to be completely overhauled." She has decided that her views are innocent and embarrassingly wholesome. All of this self-hatred she displaces onto the great collection of the Metropolitan. She's ashamed to acknowledge her indifference to Rembrandt. She wouldn't dare admit to Eisenburg that in Botticelli's *The Three Miracles of Zenobius* she likes best the human and compassionate eyes of the centurions' horses, which remind her of the eyes of her own great-uncle Graham, whom she adored. Nor would she admit that she was delighted with a Crivelli Madonna because the peaches in the background look exactly like marzipan. "While she knew that feelings like these were not really punishable, she had not perfected the air of tossing them off."

The Metropolitan should not, in theory at least, carry either a negative or a positive charge of emotion. Each art work should speak for itself. But that's not how Emma experiences the great massing of genius in the building on Fifth Avenue. She sees it as a threat to her fragile self and a weapon in the hands of her enemies. Even those of us who have loved museums all our lives, and hope to continue loving them indefinitely, will have to acknowledge that Emma, like Nathaniel Hawthorne, has a point.

The Spirit of the West
in the Jihad Era

The predicament of Western civilization is that it has ceased to be
aware of the values which it is in peril of losing. – ARTHUR KOESTLER

I t was a curious ellipsis in the global narrative of human events,
a gap in time that lasted a dozen years, 1989 to 2001, from the fall
of the Berlin Wall to the fall of the Twin Towers. In that giddy
time optimists believed that civilization had a chance to heal the
wounds of the twentieth century and create a new era of widespread
peace and prosperity.

This brief flowering of optimism found its perfect articulation in a
text that began with a discussion of Hegel's ideas and developed into
a startling account of emerging geopolitics. "The End of History?"
first appeared in the summer 1989 issue of a low-circulation journal
for conservative intellectuals, *The National Interest*. It quickly became
the most famous article of the era. It was quoted around the world,
and translated in journals from Moscow to Tokyo. People who had
never before been aware of the author's existence found themselves
earnestly discussing his thesis.

He was Francis Fukuyama, a 37-year-old philosopher and professor of government, the son of a Japanese-American sociologist who
was also a minister in the Congregational Church and the grandson
of the founder of the economics department at Kyoto University.
He had studied political philosophy with Allan Bloom in his undergraduate years at Cornell and later served as a policy planner in the
Reagan government.

Fukuyama's article, and the longer version that later appeared as a
book, suggested that we were moving toward a worldwide consensus
based on political and economic liberalism. Events were leading to
the "homogenization of all human societies," rather like the Europe
that Hegel imagined when contemplating the victories of Napoleon.

Liberal democracy, as practised in Europe, North America, and a
few other places, had proven itself the only form of political aspira-
tion capable of spanning regions and cultures across the globe: "What
we may be witnessing is not just the end of the Cold War, or the passing of a particular period of postwar history, but the end of history

AYAAN HIRSI ALI, 2015. PHOTO BY DARREN CALABRESE FOR THE GLOBE AND MAIL.

as such," perhaps "the end point of mankind's ideological evolution." Conceivably, it was "the final form of human government."

Today those words feel like a fragment of a manifesto left behind by some long-dead utopian movement. Far from expanding across the world, political and economic liberalism is under siege. Only two years ago the financial system created by the market economy was almost at the point of collapse. China has proven that a managed economy within a dictatorship can expand faster than a free market economy – at least in the short term. The Arab world has made it plain that it has no intention of adopting principles more or less dictated by the West, whatever the West offers. An article like Fukuyama's, if written today, would be regarded as at best eccentric.

No one could fault Fukuyama for his failure to anticipate the future, a common mistake in writing about politics. But he erred in another way, through a failure of imagination, an extreme case of Eurocentrism, and a limited sense of history. His article and book breathed an air of passivity. This did not occur to me in 1989, and did not appear in any of the critiques of Fukuyama I read, but it seems obvious to me now: he had forgotten the most obvious point to be learned from the ragged, uneven history of free institutions. They are created, and must be defended, through struggle, perhaps violent struggle but at minimum a long process of impassioned argument, stretching over generations. Fukuyama expected that political freedom would be spread naturally by the success of the world market. He thought, against all experience, that it would be fairly easy, even automatic.

A different idea appeared a few years later, the work of Samuel Huntington. It was formulated first in a 1992 lecture, then spelled out in a 1993 article in *Foreign Affairs*, and finally developed at length in his 1996 book *The Clash of Civilizations and the Remaking of World Order*.

Huntington recognized that the economic systems of the world were indeed coming together. That was the trouble. The power of economic integration was generating hostile reactions on religious, political, and cultural grounds. What Fukuyama saw as a success, much of the world considered a menace. Huntington argued that non-Western cultures might accept certain aspects of Western culture but did not view with equanimity the West's power. They might accept capitalism's consumer products while rejecting the West's principles, such as individual-ism and the separation of religion from the state. Secularization, so essential to the West, remains anathema in many other places, even those willing to embrace the West's economic and commercial styles.

This means, Huntington wrote in the early 1990s, that "somewhere in the Middle East a half-dozen young men could well be dressed in jeans, drinking Coke, listening to rap, and, between their bows to Mecca, putting together a bomb to blow up an American airlin-er." He believed Fukuyama too narrowly focused on economics. He predicted, correctly, that future conflicts would spring from cultural and religious differences. "The clash of civilizations will dominate global politics."

Everyone who writes and talks for a living inevitably makes mis-takes, some more painful than others. One of my mine was so egre-gious that I wince every time I think of it. Twenty years ago, invited to speak on the subject of postmodernism at the Royal Ontario Museum in Toronto, I pointed out that postmodern thought had generated a severe, wide-ranging critique of liberalism, often in the form of an at-tack on the way liberal ideas had been distorted to justify colonialism.

After my talk someone asked what effect this critique would have on liberalism. I handled that with ease: I said liberalism needed to be challenged. It would respond to postmodern arguments creatively and vigorously. It would emerge from the process refreshed, with its Enlightenment roots strengthened.

My response was dead wrong – certainly as wrong as anything Fukuyama said. During the years that followed, most sources of opin-ion (journalists, politicians, academics, trade union leaders) showed almost no interest in defending the system on which their careers and lives were based. Many signed on with the critics of the West who were far more interested in denigrating than in celebrating and buttressing the accomplishments of our civilization. I had guessed that political correctness was an outlandish fad of the 1990s. Instead it blossomed in the new century into something like a way of life, its forces installed in human rights commissions, the universities, and the editorial offices of newspapers.

The writings of the late Edward Said, and in particular his 1978

ROBERT FULFORD

book *Orientalism*, have done more than those of anyone else to
create this climate. I knew something of Said when I gave my glib
answer to the questioner at the museum, but I had no idea that in
many American, British, and Canadian universities his words were
being treated like Holy Writ. It is now assumed by his legion of
supporters (the "Church of St Edward," as Bernard Lewis has called
them) that he was altogether justified in his wholesale denunciation
of scholars in the West. They have been convicted, with a terrible
finality, of treating populations in the Middle East and other regions
as "the Other," exotic creatures to whom the rules of civilization did
not necessarily apply.

Faced with this drumbeat of Saidian opinion, most of the defend-
ers of the West have fallen silent. To judge by their writing, many
have acquired the belief that in any argument on world affairs we
should avoid at all cost taking our own side. Guilt has neutered them.
Because the West acted badly in the course of exploiting the southern
half of the planet, and because many of us have profited by this exploitation (if only through the accident of birth), we have no right to
insist on the principles the West has developed. The moral courage of
the West has grown feeble, and what we might call its moral strategy
has lost its ability to impress a large public.

Albert Camus saw this coming in the 1950s as despair over the
end of French colonialism was slowly giving birth to post-colonial
studies. Camus considered it futile to condemn several centuries of
European expansion on the basis of colonialism's crimes and failures:

> It is fitting for a nation long in tradition and with a strong
> sense of honour to find the courage to denounce its own errors.
> But it should not forget all the reasons it could still have for
> self-esteem. In any case it is dangerous to ask it to confess that
> it alone was guilty, and to doom it to perpetual penitence.

That's an opinion rarely expressed today.

Even so, a few contrary voices insist on being heard. Ibn Warraq (a
pen name for the secularist author of Pakistani origin who wrote *Why
I Am Not a Muslim* in 1995) is a remarkable example. In 2007 he wrote a

carefully detailed book, *Defending the West: A Critique of Edward Said's Orientalism*. Warraq's resourceful scholarship makes this a text that should be part of any course in which Said's ideas appear.

Warraq works through a multitude of Said's inaccuracies and selective quotations and condemns his reliance on dubious post-modern theorizing about truth. The Said arguments have done more than undermine the West's belief in itself, Warraq argues. They have also provided Middle Eastern dictatorships with a way of blaming the West for all the troubles of their national communities. "In cultures already immune to self-criticism," Warraq believes, "Said helped Muslims, and particularly Arabs, perfect their already well-developed sense of self-pity."

Pascal Bruckner, the French philosopher, has his own view of these issues. "Nothing is more Western than hatred of the West," he says in his recent book, *The Tyranny of Guilt: An Essay on Western Masochism* (2006). Twenty-first-century Euro-Americans, he writes, are supposed to have only one obligation: "endlessly atoning for what we have inflicted on other parts of humanity."

He has no patience for the belief that the West should remain silent in the face of backward and totalitarian states. Our traditions demand that we insist on the permanent relevance, in fact the universal promise, of the progress the West has made over the centuries. "The Enlightenment belongs to the entire human race," he writes – an idea that was commonplace a few decades ago but has been condemned by fashion as aggressive and arrogant.

The Arab countries have developed free-thinking minorities that deserve the West's help. Bruckner thinks we should encourage the rebels throughout the Islamic world as we supported Eastern European dissidents a generation ago. "Today there is no cause more sacred, more serious, or more pressing for the harmony of future generations." He reminds us that Kant defined the Enlightenment with a phrase, "dare to know." We need to revive the dictator-defying courage that created the freedoms we are now privileged to enjoy.

The West must find ways to deal decisively with extremist elements in resurgent Islam, everything from jihadi plots to Canadian and European Muslims who campaign to introduce sharia law into their new homelands. These problems require skill, dedication, scholarship, and uncommon patience, qualities that must be generated by the citizens.

In this historic and necessary project, one of the West's chief allies is Ayaan Hirsi Ali. This Somali-born former Muslim, now also a former Dutch parliamentarian, has for several years been doing her best to instruct us on the crisis in our communities, a crisis many among us would rather ignore.

She rejects, as sentimental and mindless, the postmodern belief that every culture is as good as any other. This is an exclusively Western idea, promulgated exclusively by people who have lived inside only one culture. She knows two. In her autobiography, *Infidel* (2006), she tells us she left the world of faith, genital cutting, and forced marriage for the world of reason and sexual emancipation. "After making this voyage I know that one of these two worlds is simply better than the other. Not for its gaudy gadgetry, but for its fundamental values."

She takes an even more radical view when she turns to religion, a sphere in which the West has opened new frontiers of pusillanimity. Violating our own most cherished principles, we have made an unwritten rule to avoid seriously challenging Islam. By common agreement this is the only faith that cannot be seriously analyzed. Europeans and North Americans, having spent centuries struggling passionately over the origins of the Hebrew Bible and the New Testament, now agree to treat the Koran with unqualified reverence.

Hirsi Ali differs. "The Koran is the work of man and not of God," she writes. "Consequently we should feel free to interpret and adapt it to modern times, rather than bending over backwards to live as the first believers did in a distant, terrible time." In those words alone she proves herself more loyal to the West than most Western intellectuals dare to be. From Somalia via Amsterdam and The Hague, the West and its friends in moderate Islam have miraculously acquired the modern champion we were unable to generate on our own.

THE CLOSING OF THE AMERICAN M·I·N·D

"An unparalleled reflection on today's intellectual and moral climate....That rarest of documents, a genuinely profound book."
The New York Times Book Review

ALLAN BLOOM

Ambassador for the Past: Allan Bloom and His Book, 25 Years Later

Whenever it enters my mind, as it often does, the name of Allan Bloom evokes, first of all, a memory of laughter. He liked to laugh, and he enjoyed laughing at himself as much as at his intellectual enemies. There was one occasion I particularly cherish, a few hours we spent together in a hotel room in Chicago a quarter of a century ago. With the *Identities* crew from TVOntario I was there to interview him for the third or fourth time. The experience of working with him was always enriching, because he had so much to say and said it with articulate, good-humoured passion. On this particular day there was something exciting and new to talk about: his life and his reputation were radically changing.

He had written an ambitious and audacious book, *The Closing of the American Mind* (1987), dealing with the place of the humanities, and especially philosophy, in American universities (it was recently reissued in a 25th anniversary edition). Unfortunately it was saddled with a clunky subtitle, *How Higher Education Has Failed Democracy and Impoverished the Souls of Today's Students*, but for some reason that did nothing to inhibit its sales.

Given the theme, Simon & Schuster started with modest expectations when they published it in February 1987. They brought out a first edition of 10,000 copies and probably would have been happy enough if they had sold just that many. But in the spring they were shocked to see sales reaching 25,000 a week.

Partly by accident, Bloom had hit on a subject many Americans, and educated people elsewhere, were worrying about: the purpose, or lack of it, in university education. Soon his book was a publishing phenomenon, on the way to selling a million copies in its various editions, more than any other book of its time by a philosopher. When this process began he was known only within the universities, and even among academics was not particularly celebrated beyond small clusters of students and colleagues. To his surprise the book would make him rich and famous and an enemy of those whose ideas he passionately opposed. It opened a new period in his life – a sadly brief period since he would die from an AIDS-related illness within five years.

That morning in Chicago he entered laughing. As soon as we said hello he began telling us that the *New York Times* had an 800 number that writers could call to determine their book's place among the bestsellers ten days before the list became generally public. He explained, in a tone that did not want to be believed, that he was of course above such grubby concerns, but someone at the publishing house had called on his behalf and learned he was in fact moving two notches up the list the following week.

Money was pouring in. It was like a folk tale or a newspaper feature on a lottery winner. To Bloom it sounded like a joke: "Man renounces all worldly desires, devotes himself to philosophy, gets rich." Later he had another line, "I'm in political philosophy because that's where the big bucks are." I've never seen anyone enjoy success so much, or anyone so amused by the spectacle of his own reactions to it. In the eyes of a philosopher, success was meaningless. In the eyes of a human being it was at once both satisfying and ridiculous.

I never knew him well, but in our several meetings I came to understand why so many of his students loved him, competed for his attention, and called him, decades later, the great teacher of their lives – sometimes, in fact, the great event of their lives or even the great event of their era.

When he made a point his dark eyes flashed; his hands gestured like errant wings, and his words expressed urgency without ever slipping into bombast.

He always had a coterie of followers, people who studied with him and followed him from lecture to lecture, then sometimes drank coffee with him later. It was clear to me that they felt more alive in his presence than otherwise. It was as if every moment in his life carried vital importance or serious enjoyment.

This intensity somehow flowed toward everyone who spent time around him. There were many people who weren't sure what he did, or why he did it, but felt nevertheless that they were in the presence of someone significant. Bloom wanted to be loved and respected. Thinking back after he was gone, I began to guess that in some sense his manner must have been self-consciously cultivated. He must have worked on it, the way a writer will work on style until he finds the tone that is uniquely his own. Nothing so fine as Bloom's way of speaking comes into existence by accident. He once expressed his view of his own style through his favourite composer. He told a friend that he wanted to be like one of the solo voices in Mozart's French horn concertos: bluff, gruff, forthright, faintly comic, yet capable of beguiling sonorities.

A friend of mine, who studied with him as an undergraduate during his years at the University of Toronto in the 1970s, remembers being surprised when she first heard someone say his book had made him famous. "I always thought he was famous," she says. "He had the manner of someone famous." He was, among other things, probably the best-dressed philosophy professor in North America. He seemed always to have a Cuban cigar. And of course everyone listened when he spoke, as they will do when someone is famous.

Clifford Orwin of the University of Toronto studied with Bloom at Cornell in the 1960s; they were colleagues at Toronto in the 1970s. In 1993 Orwin wrote a memoir of Bloom for *The American Scholar* and included this beautiful tribute:

> *He had the gift of making us feel that study was something exalted, one of the rarest human privileges, for the opportunity of which we should never cease to be thankful....*
> *Through knowing him it suddenly became credible that a life devoted to studying a couple of dozen mostly old books was one of surpassing nobility and joyfulness; in him we actually saw this life before us, and, however fleetingly, joined in it.*

Many admiring reviews greeted *The Closing of the American Mind*, but in time the negative reviews grew more numerous and far more emphatic. In the eyes of many people in his profession, Bloom had done something terrible. Reviewers saw him as an authoritarian menace. David Rieff called him "vengeful, reactionary, anti-democratic," the author of a book that "decent people would be ashamed of having written." Martha Nussbaum in the *New York Review of Books* gave a ruling as if from on high: Bloom could not even be called a philosopher, much less a good one. Many agreed that he was an elitist, and this was itself a bad thing to be. Louis Menand, in his review for the *New Republic*, gave one possible reason for the book's success: "It gratifies our wish to think ill of our culture (a wish that is a permanent feature of modernity) without thinking ill of ourselves."

Early in 1988 I was working at University College in the University of Toronto. A philosophy professor, whom I'd never seen before, approached me one day to ask why in the world I would interview "a man like" Allan Bloom on television. I said I had found his book enlightening and asked if he didn't think there was something to be said for it. He replied that he hadn't read it but knew it was bad. It turned out that he hadn't seen the TV interview, either. He preferred instead to be guided by what was in the air. Another philosophy professor told me Bloom was a fascist; apparently he had proven this by criticizing feminism.

There was worse to come. On September 25, 1988, the *New York Times* reported on a humanities conference, jointly held by Duke University and the University of North Carolina, at which Bloom's work had been enthusiastically derided and laughed at by speaker after speaker. Richard Bernstein, the reporter, wrote that the scene recalled the daily "Two Minutes Hate" in George Orwell's *Nineteen Eighty-Four* (1949), when citizens rose together to hurl invective at the Great Enemy of the state. Bloom's real sin, it developed, was his lack of enthusiasm for egalitarian liberalism as it affected the life of the university. A student of Leo Strauss, he had absorbed the belief that philosophers naturally view political systems with suspicion. Now he saw the American ethos of the late twentieth century swamping the standard university curriculum and depriving students of the life-enhancing wisdom that he, and many generations before him, had taken for granted. Like everyone else, he could see that with each day the place of the humanities in the universities grew slightly less significant. Just as the humanities had taken over much of the space given to religion in earlier versions of the university, they were being forced to surrender their own position to several competitors, all of them steadily increasing in power and prestige: the sciences, the professions, the social sciences, and the business schools.

Bloom, naturally, found this disquieting. But his feelings were mixed. He realized that part of the trouble was self-inflicted. The study of literature had fallen under the sway of politicized theory that made it worse than useless to most students. And philosophy had given itself over to a relativism that undermined the search for truth, philosophy's central function. He wasn't at all sure that the humanities, as they existed in the last few decades of his life, deserved a vigorous defence.

The word "closing" in his title expressed his view that education was now delivering the opposite of what it promised. Universities had dedicated themselves "to the new educational dawn called openness, a dawn whose rosy fingers are currently wrapped tightly around the throat of the curriculum in most universities." This openness was in fact a mindless relativism: "Openness used to be the virtue that permitted us to seek the good by using reason. It now means accepting everything and denying reason's power." A "nonelitist" curriculum in the humanities meant that the classic texts were to be studied as expressions of "the unconscious class, gender or race prejudices of their authors." The humanities could now liberate us from the prejudices of people such as Shakespeare and Milton. Humanists, rather than learning from the old books, would dedicate themselves to battling against Eurocentrism. Students would be taught to unlearn the value of these books before they learned what the books could teach.

My title is a quote from Orwin's article; he saw that Bloom, as an ambassador for the past, made a point of introducing his students to history, including recent history. In talking to Bloom I gathered that he wanted most of all to teach students how they could intellectually free themselves from the tyranny of the present. He wanted them to know they didn't have to think the way everyone around them was thinking. The young can easily become provincial in regard to time; they believe the moment they inhabit is the most important one – in the 1960s they often sensed that it was somehow endowed with more wisdom than any earlier time. He wanted students to be comfortable also in the older world, the one he inhabited, where Plato and Rousseau talked to each other as Michelangelo looked on. He saw university closing off this possibility, in the name of egalitarianism.

Accused of Eurocentrism and a perverse regard for the works of dead white men, Bloom quoted what W.E.B. DuBois said in 1903 in his book, *The Souls of Black Folk* :

> *I sit with Shakespeare and he winces not. Across the color line I move arm in arm with Balzac and Dumas.... From out of the caves of evening that swing between the strong-limbed earth and the tracery of the stars, I summon Aristotle and Aurelius and what soul I will, and they come all graciously with no scorn or condescension.*

It was Saul Bellow (also foolishly accused, from time to time, of elitism) who listened to his friend Bloom talk for many years and then urged him to write *The Closing of the American Mind*, for which Bellow then provided an enthusiastic foreword. And in 2000, eight years after Bloom's death, it was Bellow who built a suitable monument to him by recreating him as Abe Ravelstein and placing him at the centre of *Ravelstein*, his last work of fiction.

That book not only sets down a great writer's account of Bloom in everything from his conversation to his clothes and the shape of his head ("that bald, cranial watchtower") but also places him perfectly in the midst of a now distant moment in intellectual history, the moment that led directly to our own. Perhaps that's what seems most important to me about Bloom's book today. He didn't live to see the unfolding of the full craziness of political correctness, but he saw it coming and understood its causes and the harm it could do to us. And his readers were at least prepared to understand it when it arrived and poisoned the air of freedom.

When I Was Very Young

Often, in someone's home or in a public building, I have the unsettling experience of coming by accident upon a painting made in Toronto during the 1950s by a member of Painters Eleven or by one of the artists, such as Michael Snow or Graham Coughtry, who were part of the circle clustered around the Isaacs Gallery. Even if the painting happens to be something I didn't much admire at the time it was made, it now touches me instantly on two levels. It's a historical artefact, and I have an urgent impulse to explain who made it and why, an impulse sometimes satisfied by answering the questions of young academics studying the period. That's part of everyday experience for me now, and it's not unusual. Much of my life, after all, has been spent "placing" cultural objects in context.

But a painting from that era also has a way of evoking ancient emotions I still feel. Late in life one understands that everything we have lived through remains in some sense lodged in an eternal present. Time doesn't erase itself; it accumulates. One's sense of how one felt as something happened never altogether disappears and often recurs in ways that shoot to the centre of consciousness. When I was very young these artists were sometimes my teachers, often my friends, always among my favourite subjects. Even now I can't imagine seeing them with anything like objectivity.

On February 13, 1954, the date of the first Painters Eleven exhibition, I turned 22. As a birthday treat a colleague took me to see their show at the Roberts Gallery on Yonge Street, which was then one of a very few commercial art galleries in Toronto. It was a hugely successful evening in some ways, not so successful in others. The crowd was the biggest ever seen at the Roberts, so big that you couldn't see the paintings. I ended up with no more than a vague general impression of swirls and brilliant colours. I remember that no one stopped talking about this new and unprecedented art; it was art that most people had never seen or had seen only in magazines from New York. But not one painting in that show was sold. People in Toronto were prepared to be excited by abstract art. They were not prepared to embrace it and take it home. That wouldn't happen till several years in the future.

This art emerged from a Canada radically different from the
one we live in now. Technology has of course changed; the ethnic
make-up of our country has changed; our place in world affairs
has changed, and the place of women has profoundly changed. (In
that regard Painters Eleven was remarkably progressive. It had two
women members, which was two more than the federal cabinet, the
executive suite of the CBC, or the Supreme Court of Canada, to name
three notable institutions.)

Beyond all those transformations, an even more fundamental
change has taken place. In 1953 we were, in political matters, a
relatively conflict-free society. Prime Minister Louis St. Laurent,
for example, was not at all what we now think a prime minister or a
premier should be. He was a quiet-spoken corporate lawyer, 65 years
old when he became prime minister in 1948 and 75 when the voters
retired him in 1957. There was little about him that was contentious
or charismatic; nor did he appear to have an agenda to promote, as
later prime ministers, such as Trudeau and Mulroney, did. He treated
government as a problem of management, to be handled smoothly
and without fuss. If anyone had called him a passionate believer in
something, other than Canada, he would have been offended. He
was a calm man for a calm era and ran his cabinet as a chairman of
the board. He left business issues to his trade minister, C.D. Howe,
an American-born engineer, and foreign affairs to Lester B. Pearson.
He had other men for finance and national defence, and he seldom
interfered with them. Canadians were apparently content to let these
quiet managers run the country. In 1953 we gave St. Laurent his second overwhelming majority.

In the mid-1950s I became an art critic, anointed first by a local CBC station and then by the *Toronto Star*. At the *Star* I wrote a
Saturday column on art and, on weekdays, reviewed books. The art
column was far less difficult than it would be today. Now a full-time
critic can't begin to review all the galleries in Toronto; indeed, it
would be a chore just to count them. But in those long-ago days I
could cover all the new shows of the week, no more than two or three
of them, on a Thursday afternoon, then write my Saturday column
on Thursday night.

Art, whether abstract or not, was in those days nothing like the vital part of sophisticated life that it seems to be today. Painting and sculpture were surrounded by mists of public indifference and even hostility. Within the art community, small as it was, certain tensions were almost institutionalized. Young artists, such as Painters Eleven, considered it obligatory to regard the Ontario College of Art with disdain or resentment. They believed they stood for the future and the college for the past. Yet as I got to know them – artists such as Harold Town, William Ronald, Michael Snow, Graham Coughtry – I began to understand how much they had learned there. At the college, some of those artists had found the guides who pointed the way to their real work, as William Ronald found his teacher, Jock Macdonald (both of them became members of Painters Eleven). Others, such as Coughtry and Snow and even Town, would slowly reveal that the college had enriched them in significant ways. In that sense the college added to my own education by teaching me that even the most highly aware of my fellow citizens can misunderstand the nature of their own experience. They learned so well that they didn't know they had learned anything at all. By accident or not, the college taught them to be independent of it.

But while they regarded the college as an implacable enemy, the artists turned most of their rage against other artists. At the centre of the battle were the old art associations, above all the Ontario Society of Artists. As Town said a couple of decades later, it gave young artists "something to aim at, to denigrate, to disparage, to try and supersede."

The OSA's main function was to organize a carefully juried annual exhibition at the Art Gallery of Ontario, which was then called the Art Gallery of Toronto. Today it would be impossible to convey how much that one exhibition meant. Artists who were accepted believed that it justified the labour of the previous year and reinforced their position in the community, especially in the schools where many of them were teaching. Artists who were rejected felt they had been annihilated, cast into outer darkness.

Many artists were regularly rejected because they were considered too experimental, immature, or even fraudulent. The OSA was considered conservative and timid. The artists who founded Painters Eleven did so partly as a way of elbowing into the official art world of Toronto – Jack Bush, one of the ringleaders and the man who kept the minutes at Painters Eleven meetings, described the founding of their group as a "power play." The OSA having more or less ignored them, they would start their own institution, in which they could not be ignored – and their eventual triumph was that they became better known than the OSA itself.

Meanwhile, the OSA boiled over with furious interior controversies. A few abstract artists, or friends of abstract artists, had made their way into it, and they were fighting with the traditionalists. At one point some rejected artists decided to hold a counter-exhibition, a Salon des Refusés, such as Manet and his colleagues had set up in Paris in the nineteenth century as a way to defy the academy. Our rebels were a little confused, though. They decided they would have a jury for their Salon des Refusés. I, being considered an up-and-coming critic, was asked to sit on the jury. Without much thought, I accepted. Within the next 24 hours someone pointed out to the rebellious artists that in its very nature a Salon des Refusés could not be juried, since that would make the paintings accepted and therefore no longer Refusés. The jury was eliminated, and I gratefully withdrew. But I tell this story to suggest that we were groping our way toward some understanding of how such things worked.

There was no Big Bang that started the abstract version of modern art in Toronto, certainly nothing like the Refus Global manifesto issued in Montreal in 1948. Abstraction crept into southern Ontario on little cat's feet, as Carl Sandburg said of fog. That first show of Painters Eleven in 1954 didn't receive even one critique, favourable or unfavourable, in the newspapers. Painters Eleven offered eleven different kinds of abstraction, but they had in common the baked energy of movement and the poetry of gesture that made abstraction the dominant form of that period. The members seemed a generation older than I, mainly because they were apparently so sure about what they wanted to accomplish. Actually, the youngest, Kazuo Nakamura and William Ronald, were my seniors by only six years. The oldest, on the other hand, Hortense Gordon, was 45 years older than I.

What were they like, these artists who made their revolution? I never knew Alexandra Luke, the woman who was responsible for convening the first meetings of Painters Eleven in her Oshawa studio. I think of her as brisk, efficient, and highly talented; I have a watercolour of hers in my kitchen, and it seems to sum up, in its delicate combination of chaos and order, the goals of abstraction in the 1950s.

Jock Macdonald, a gentle and mystical Scotsman, was one artist who progressed through two famous schools of painting in Canada. In Vancouver, a student and friend of Fred Varley, he painted in a style that echoed the Group of Seven; later, in Toronto, he became an abstract artist and for the first time made paintings that were highly personal and met the high standards he was setting for himself. When I knew him he seemed older than the 57 or 58 he was, perhaps because of wounds suffered in the First World War.

Nakamura was a sly, small, enigmatic fellow who never spoke more than two sentences in succession. His bible was *Scientific American*, and on the first occasion when I interviewed him he brought out a copy of it and showed me a photograph of cell structure that was inspiring his current work. He was perhaps the most confidently purposeful of all these artists, yet the least articulate. He quietly pursued his own style in his own way and left an impressive and delicate body of work. Tom Hodgson was an individual I wrote about at two different stages of his life and mine. I started in newspaper work as a sports writer and covered a powerful young Olympic canoeist, Tom Hodgson. A few years later I found myself writing about the same young man as a talented member of Painters Eleven.

Hodgson was profoundly affected by the most traumatic event in the years when the Eleven were exhibiting, the sudden death of Oscar Cahén in an automobile accident in 1956. Cahén was a wonderfully imaginative painter, a highly successful commercial artist, and a broadly cultured European. His death robbed the others of a natural leader.

Bush, who spent much of his life as an advertising art director, was a grey-flannel executive with a moustache and the polished manner of a man accustomed to impressing clients. In the 1970s his beauti-

fully constructed abstractions ended up making a larger impact on
international art than the work of anyone else in Canada.

William Ronald was a great bull of a man, bitter and resentful, so
narrowly focused on his status that it was hard to get him to speak of
anything else. He loved to threaten critics. In 1970, after one negative
review, Ronald phoned the critic (I think it was Barry Lord), announced that he was a violent man, and said that if they were ever in
the same room, he couldn't be responsible for his actions. Nine years
later, the phone rang in my own house at 3 a.m. It was Ronald, drunk,
threatening to come over and beat me up for a piece I had written in
Saturday Night magazine on Painters Eleven.

I was puzzled, since I'd written not a single word against him.
My crime, it turned out, was saying that Jack Bush was the only
member of the group who now had an international reputation. This
implied, accurately, that Ronald had been forgotten in New York
since the 1950s. Even after two decades, he wasn't accepting that fact.
Somehow, he forgot to come over and beat me up.

He never failed to make an impression. Invited to lecture at
Princeton, he strode on stage and painted a picture before the audience while a tape played jazz in the background. In the late 1960s, I
was chairing a University of Toronto panel discussion. Ronald didn't
show up at the appointed time, so we assumed he had forgotten and
went ahead without him. He hadn't forgotten. He was just waiting
to make an entrance. After a few minutes, while another speaker was
delivering his profundities, Ronald strode in, wearing a sweeping
blue cape, a Viking helmet, and gigantic boots. He didn't like to go
unnoticed.

Ronald and his younger brother lived out the strangest story
in Canadian painting of their time, a story still largely untold.
They were two excellent artists from the same family, a circumstance
familiar in music but comparatively rare in painting. They were
small-town Ontario boys, bearing the plainest names anyone ever
heard, Bill Smith and John Smith. The sons of a factory worker
in Brampton, they both studied at the Ontario College of Art.
Professionally, both used only their first and middle names:
Bill became William Ronald and John, seven years younger, became

John Meredith. Ronald died in 1998, and Meredith's death in 2000 brought their story to an end.

It was a melancholy story, because for all their talent they were miserable and angry men, and especially angry at each other. Their mutual antagonism went far beyond the normal resentments of siblings working in the same profession. They didn't speak for years at a time, and neither of them liked hearing anyone mention the other.

In a strange way the art world respected their privacy in this matter. Essays on Meredith rarely speculated on the possible influence of his older brother. When Robert Belton was writing *The Theatre of the Self: The Life and Art of William Ronald* (1999), he couldn't pry a word about Meredith out of Ronald. Belton couldn't get anything useful from Meredith, either, and the astonishing result is a painter's biography that barely mentions the existence of a painter sibling.

Harold Town I knew best. He suggested the name, Painters Eleven, and wrote the little notes that were published on the invitations to their shows. He was famously voluble, astoundingly pleased with his work, and totally incapable of telling a good Harold Town from a bad Harold Town (in that he resembled the poet Irving Layton). There was nothing on which Town was not an expert, at least in his own eyes, and certainly he was better read in many fields than most painters. Naturally he and Ronald, being equally wrathful and roughly the same age, started their own private war within the walls of Painters Eleven, a war that lasted several decades. Most outsiders never understood its causes but never doubted its vehemence.

In 1955 I interviewed Hortense Gordon, born in 1887, easily the oldest non-objective painter in Canada. She was 68 that year. I could hardly believe that this quiet, modest woman, so much like a grandmother in my eyes, striking only for her black wig, was among those who had embarked on what still seemed an outrageously challenging kind of work, painting with no subject.

Wassily Kandinsky's first experiments along these lines were four decades old, but few of his paintings had ever been exhibited here. In the newspaper world I inhabited while trying to learn cultural history in my spare time, abstract painting was generally considered to be some sort of minor joke perpetrated by artists who might fool some part of the public for a brief period but would no doubt vanish from sight in another few years, like most fads.

What could the artists (and their supporters, like me) pit against that heedless philistinism? What did we have on our side? We had arrogance. We believed we knew what should be done – and we really believed we knew what should not be done, which was the traditionalist art promoted by the OSA and the college. We chose our enemies, and fought in the usual way, with an uncoordinated but effective combination of private sneers and public declarations of principle.

In the catalogue for the exhibition 1953, organized at the Robert McLaughlin Gallery in Oshawa in 2003, Ihor Holubizky wrote: "Every generation declares and invents its own independence." In my experience this usually means ignoring the generations that have come before and the battles they have fought. Gathering enough confidence to do anything of value is a major project for most artists, and it's often necessary to believe that you are starting with a blank slate. Canadian writers of each generation have traditionally believed that no writing of consequence was produced in this country till they came along.

But by the 1950s Canadian painters were unable to share this particular form of blindness. They could hardly ignore the Group of Seven, which was as omnipresent then as it is now. Several members were living among us, still producing. For a young painter it was necessary somehow to come to terms with the Group of Seven. You could condemn them as provincial, which implied that you were not. You could suggest that they were only an isolated moment in history, casting no influence into the future, which implied that you carried the future in your bones. You could even suggest that they had exhausted their subject. Graham Coughtry resented the way he was stuffed with Group of Seven art in school. He made the much-quoted statement that "Every damn tree in this country has been painted."

That was a common opinion. But over the years many of the artists of that generation slowly changed their views. Town told me in the 1950s that nothing about the Group of Seven and their time interested him; but decades later he became the co-author of a loving book about Tom Thomson. Michael Snow used the Group's art in a work he did for an exhibition in Paris, and many other painters have discovered that the Group has something to say to them, too. But in the 1950s, among young or youngish artists, this was not a popular opinion.

Something I call "pride of period" causes us to believe that we have better answers to the crucial questions than our ancestors; every era imagines it has reached a fresh level of wisdom. It's a kind of collective intoxication. We become drunk on our ideas. In the 1950s those who spent their lives around art were perhaps particularly inebriated. It's this feeling that rushes back to me whenever I happen upon an early Snow or Ronald.

Abstraction was our drink of choice, and the New York School of abstract expressionists was our favourite distillery. Just a few years earlier the centre of gravity in world art had shifted from Paris to New York, and in the 1950s we were still dealing with this astonishing fact, something that no one in the world had anticipated.

There's something exhilarating about pride of period. It creates currents of energy on which we ride, but there's almost always something quite mad about it as well. If we were all a little mad in the 1950s we can perhaps find an excuse in the fact that a brilliant writer in New York was leading us toward this lunacy.

Clement Greenberg was a formalist in the strictest sense, believing that we should see a painting as only a painting, not a window onto something else and certainly not a commentary on the world. Jackson Pollock, abandoning every element of objective reality, was the artist Greenberg first loved and championed.

Greenberg believed there was no going back to representation; that way, he argued, lay sentimental, vulgar, hackneyed art. In 1939 he imported into the discussion of the arts the German word "kitsch," which he defined as "vicarious experience and faked sensations." He considered kitsch to be "the epitome of all that is spurious in the life of our times." Art had to go forward because, as he put it, "The alternative to Picasso is not Michelangelo but kitsch."

Greenberg played a large role in the life of Painters Eleven. They all knew about him, talked about him, and finally got up the nerve to bring him to Toronto to look at their work. He visited their studios, talked encouragingly with most of them, showed a particular interest in the work of William Ronald, and formed a permanent bond with Jack Bush.

He helped Bush find a dealer in New York, helped him choose which pictures to show, and even advised him on what course his art should take. He became his coach, and after Bush's death he was a careful, thoughtful executor of his estate.

Greenberg was the twentieth century's most influential critic, like John Ruskin in the nineteenth century. One reason was his enormous confidence. He had been a Marxist for some years; he had abandoned Marxist beliefs, but he had retained the confidence that was always the most obvious characteristic of Marxists.

In that way, Marxists are like Anglicans. We Anglicans may lose our faith, but we retain our prejudices and our attitudes, sometimes even our Anglican tone of voice. In the same way, Greenberg ceased to be a Marxist but retained a Marxist's belief in the inevitability of history. He just transferred it from politics to art. His tone was dogmatic and combative because he knew that history was on his side. He said to artists, in effect: here is the mainstream, it runs from Cubism through Matisse and Mondrian to Pollock and onward. Everything else is irrelevant – surrealism, Pop Art, political art, and all the rest.

When I think about Greenberg and others of his time, it occurs to me that even the desires of the world have gone into reverse since 1953. Today we celebrate the broadening of aesthetics, the opening up of art and communication to all conceivable impulses. But the era around 1953 was a time of narrowing. When I went to design conferences I heard people issuing strict rules about how materials were to be used. In the most fashionable homes of the young, all the design was from Scandinavia, where designers worked with a narrow palette, bland colours and a few beautifully grained woods.

In ambitious architecture, the regulations of Ludwig Mies van der Rohe were famously strict; no decoration, straight lines, square corners, acres of glass. Everyone who pronounced on these subjects seemed anxious to limit what was permissible. And of course Greenberg, by far the most articulate writer on any of these subjects, was better than anyone else at limiting what he considered appropriate. Northrop Frye, in one of his journals, called this "the illusion of raising one's standards by limiting one's sympathies."

Greenberg was so persuasive that he almost literally blinded his followers. There was a moment, in 1965, when it became briefly possible to see the comic aspect of his dogma with sudden clarity. That was when it moved outside the art milieu and into a courtroom, during a famous obscenity trial. *Eros 65*, an exhibition of Canadian erotic art at the Dorothy Cameron Gallery on Yonge Street, led to Cameron being charged with obscenity under the Criminal Code. Police swooped down and singled out work by Robert Markle and several other painters, issuing subpoenas and seizing the paintings. Now at this time Harold Town considered himself just about the sexiest painter in Canada if not the known world. But the police ignored his contributions to the Cameron show and subpoenaed the work of others. It was said that for a long time afterward Harold suffered from subpoena envy.

I attended the trial, where the works of art were on exhibit. They explicitly showed various sexual acts, in what I thought was an agreeable way and the police thought was despicable. What was fascinating, though, was the difference between the art works themselves and what the witnesses for the defence said about them. Witnesses, all from the art community, came forward one after another and stated under oath that, despite the clear evidence of our eyes, these art works were not in fact concerned with sex but rather were exercises in the play of light and shadow, abstract form, etc. Knowingly or not, these people were all Greenbergian formalists. They believed form mattered, not subject; therefore they couldn't see the subject. As the witnesses made this absolutely ludicrous statement in all seriousness, the magistrate watched them, incredulous, apparently finding it hard to believe that anyone would try to get away with such nonsense.

He found Dorothy Cameron guilty, and by implication cast doubt on the credibility of the witnesses, but they were not dissembling – they had become so infatuated with abstract ideas about art that they sincerely believed the drawings they were looking at mainly depicted volume, density, the play of light and shadow, etc.

In those ancient and now dimly remembered disputes, did Greenberg know where art was going? Did Painters Eleven? No, and no. Greenberg had no idea that art, far from following his narrowly formalist plan, would spread in a dozen different directions – toward political art and minimalism and earth art and installations and video. These were tendencies Greenberg glimpsed but turned away from in horror. He dismissed them as irrelevancies or "strategies," meaning ways to get attention. As for Painters Eleven, they were right in the sense that they knew what they should do and did it well, but wrong to consider it was the wave of the future, the only one. It was a movement, a great movement, but only a single movement, and one that soon lost much of its potency and all of its claim to dominance.

I shouldn't be surprised that things turned out this way, or disappointed. Nor should I let a little thing like the course of civilization inhibit the pleasure I take from remembering those long-ago events and feelings. The future is always unforeseeable, perhaps especially for those who believe they are creating it.

105,683. JV

The Race, Don Valley,
Toronto, Canada.

In Atwood's Toronto

VIEW OF DON VALLEY, TORONTO. POSTCARD C. 1910

In the first sentence of Margaret Atwood's novel, *The Blind Assassin*, a beautiful 25-year-old woman kills herself by driving off the St. Clair Avenue bridge, east of Mount Pleasant Road. The car smashes through "the treetops feathery with new leaves," and Laura Chase quickly burns to death on the floor of the ravine, 100 feet below.

This is a Toronto death, and a literary death, and a death charged with symbolic power for both the character and the woman who has created her. It stands at the narrative gate of Atwood's 10th novel, which opens on to scenes of psychic horror, monstrous oppression and betrayal – not to mention a clever plot that includes both a novel within a novel and also a third novel, a science-fiction fantasy set on the planet Zycron. This innermost story, a perverse and sadistic tale, is told within the realistic love story that one of Atwood's characters is writing.

Atwood, we can be sure, did not choose the locale of the suicide casually. It fits into her book and into her life's work by underscoring once more her intense relationship with Toronto and its folklore. For a long time she's been a grand international figure, loved by the Germans, the English, the Japanese, and God knows who else, and of course admired across the United States and Canada. Even so, we who live in Toronto maintain a special relationship with her. As Mark Abley noted in *The Guardian*, "Toronto looks on her with fond possessiveness." Any Atwood narrator would immediately identify that phrase as a veiled threat, but the truth is that she's become, more than anyone else, our novelist, the intimate chronicler of our lives, true successor to Robertson Davies as chief mythologist of Toronto life, past as well as present.

In 1972 Atwood wrote, "Literature is not only a mirror, it is also a map, a geography of the mind." Her fiction maps Toronto, its geography and its psychology; she's our urban cartographer. As the years pass and the books pile up, she beavers away at the job of understanding Toronto and describing, in her oblique ways, the specific individuals and human types who walk its streets and explore its ravines. She's conscious of her responsibilities, and meticulous about her Toronto facts: After she wrote her opening suicide scene, she sent a researcher to determine that the drop from the bridge actually measures 100 feet. More than any other living writer, she's rooted in Toronto – if not always in Toronto reality, then certainly in her own carefully formed construct of the city.

She turns Laura's suicide into a specifically and uniquely Toronto event by placing it over a ravine. Ravines are the chief characteristic of the local terrain, its topographical signature. They are both a tangible (though often hidden) part of our surroundings and a persistent force in our civic imagination. They are the shared subconscious of the municipality, the places where much of the city's literature is born.

Laura's decision to die in the Vale of Avoca, close to Rosedale, fits the story and reflects her tragedy. The life from which she's making a final definitive escape is a specifically Rosedale life, and it has destroyed her soul. The evil spirits living behind the elegant facades on Rosedale's winding streets shape the action in *The Blind Assassin*, and Laura is their victim. (The book contains rich people and poor people; readers may guess which group is irredeemably ruthless and vile.)

The death scene also takes place only a few blocks west and south of the street on the edge of Leaside where Margaret Atwood herself discovered the power of ravines. In 1948, when she was nine, her family settled near the southeastern corner of Mount Pleasant Cemetery. At the end of the street behind her house, a footbridge led toward a patch of the peculiar ravine wildness that defines Toronto, especially for children. As Rosemary Sullivan says in her book *The Red Shoes: Margaret Atwood Starting Out*, "Margaret could climb down through dense underbrush into the Moore Park Ravine, which snaked through the east side of the city" – and connected directly with the setting of Laura's death. Sullivan quotes Atwood's note on the ravines, written years later: "To go down into them is to go down into sleep, away from the conscious electrified life of the houses. The ravines are darker, even in the day."

Beneath the bridge, where Laura dies, the streams trickle toward the Don River, Toronto's literary corridor. The Don is the Euphrates of Toronto books, home of our myths and legends. Head to the east and you find yourself in Ernest Thompson Seton territory, where that great Victorian naturalist (a favourite of Atwood's in childhood) did the private exploring that led to his classics, *Wild Animals I Have Known* and *Two Little Savages*. Follow the ravine south from the St. Clair bridge as it joins the Don proper and soon you'll reach Bloor Street, where (with a little imagination) you can see Michael Ondaatje's characters from *In the Skin of a Lion* (1987) completing the construction of the Bloor viaduct in the 1930s. Keep going and you can glimpse, on the east bank that forms Riverdale Park, the lovers and dreamers who populate the young Morley Callaghan's novels of the 1920s, like *It's Never Over* (1930), that intense account of claustrophobic urban frustration. Move on south to Gerrard and Dundas, glance to your right, and there are Hugh Garner's defeated Cabbage-town dwellers, sitting on the grassy slopes as they endure the Depression and wonder whether to volunteer for the war in Spain. Not far away, you'll run into the male protagonist of Catherine Bush's 1993 novel, *Minus Time*, that wonderfully Toronto-centric book; he tells us that as a 13-year-old he ran away from home and lived in the ravines, becoming briefly famous in the papers as Ravine Boy. Keep going far enough, reach the lake, make a right, and eventually you can find a major Robertson Davies character, Boy Staunton from *Fifth Business* (1970), dead at the bottom of Toronto harbour, sitting in his Cadillac convertible, his mouth inexplicably filled with a large chunk of pink granite. (Is Laura's automobile suicide a 30-years-later echo of Boy's?)

Atwood's self-chosen assignment is to pull together the folk tales of Toronto, compiling and ordering all our myths and clichés and prejudices, packaging them as neatly (but in her own way) as those two German brothers did in *Grimm's Fairy Tales* (1812), the book Atwood once cited as the most influential in her life. *Lady Oracle* (1976), *Life Before Man* (1979), *The Robber Bride* (1993), *Alias Grace* (1996) and *The Blind Assassin* (2000) – these are all elaborations on Atwood's vision of her city and its surroundings.

Pursuing the obsessions of her Torontonians naturally takes Atwood into the ravines. In *Lady Oracle*, Joan describes her childhood trauma suffered in a ravine. In *Cat's Eye* (1988), that painfully brilliant account of the viciousness of children, a ravine is where Cordelia tortures her alleged friend, Elaine. Here, in the secrecy of the trees, away from the eyes of teachers and parents, the girls can mistreat each other at will, in an Atwoodian female version of *Lord of the Flies* (1954)

Even when her characters are rooted elsewhere, their stories carry them to Toronto. The two women at the centre of *The Blind Assassin* are from a small town in southwestern Ontario, something like Stratford, and one of them, the wordy octogenarian narrator, spends most of her life there. But they act out both the terrible and the ecstatic moments of their existence in Toronto.

Atwood has been cast in the role of feminist by popular mythology and by the often combative tone of her work, especially her poetry. But Atwoodian fiction rarely follows a feminist line. Certainly she's sensitive to the spirit of the moment, but it clearly matters more to her that she remain honest to humanity as she sees it. In the environment she knows best, the success-focused arena of Toronto, feminist pieties don't apply. In this angry, driven world, an unwritten law of envy decrees that every success must be followed by a reaction of equal and opposite resentment. Atwood, being the writer she is, could hardly ignore the truth that women follow the rules of this world as slavishly as men – just as, decades ago, she demonstrated that Atwood the Nationalist could never be allowed to prevent Atwood the Novelist from seeing and depicting the inherent comedy in certain attitudes of her fellow nationalists.

Unfortunately, the girls in *Cat's Eye* do not necessarily change when they grow up; woman's inhumanity to woman remains a fact that no rhetoric can erase. In a 1993 *Maclean's* review of *The Robber Bride*, Judith Timson shrewdly remarked: "As a sort of grown-up sequel to Atwood's 1988 novel, *Cat's Eye*, the book seems to be saying that if you think little girls can be mean to each other, you should see what big ones can accomplish." In a single heart-stopping moment that defines the book's title, *The Blind Assassin* repeats this pattern. Typically for Atwood, this 1945 conversation takes place in one of the temples of propriety that were typical of the Old Toronto, Diana Sweets.

Like all novelists, Atwood draws her characters from the people around her, and ends up (rather like Davies) with a gallery of frequently recognizable Toronto figures. She avoids the more or less strict system of the roman à clef as famously exemplified by Simone de Beauvoir's *The Mandarins* (1954), in which great names in French intellectual life of the 1950s (Jean-Paul Sartre, Albert Camus, etc.) were simply given different names and allowed to follow just about the same course they followed in life (as de Beauvoir later explained in her autobiographical writing).

Atwood's strategy is different. She unravels the fabric of her Toronto, or the Toronto she knows at the moment of writing, and then reknits it in a new form, drawing emotional strength and human detail from experience and observation while stamping them as her own.

This is not to say she makes them unrecognizable. In *The Robber Bride*, for instance, more than one reader recognized a grotesque version of Barbara Amiel and a fanciful elaboration on Atwood's late friend, the poet Gwendolyn MacEwen. But it was in *Life Before Man*, that powerful (and powerfully chilling) account of her Toronto in the 1970s, that Atwood most clearly relied on living models. There she took a group of people who had known each other at the House of Anansi Press and moved them into the Royal Ontario Museum, a place Atwood haunted as a child and later wrote poetry about. *Life Before Man* contains versions of Atwood, her former husband and her life's partner, Graeme Gibson. Elizabeth, the most fascinating figure in the story, both repellent and alluring, seems to many people based on Gibson's former wife, Shirley Gibson. Certainly she thought so, and spoke of a libel action until calmer heads prevailed. Perhaps she realized that you do not sue over fiction without making yourself ridiculous.

In a small way, I have been part of Atwood's Toronto, as an occasional editor of her magazine work, the subject of one of her articles long ago, and sometimes a reviewer of her books or a critic of her politics. In 1988, in a book of memoirs, I included a passage about her that I considered more admiring than not but she regarded otherwise. In 1990 she wrote a story, "Uncles," originally published in *Saturday Night* magazine, expressing her displeasure. She included it in her collection *Wilderness Tips* (1991), and in England a review by Anita Brookner summarized it as the account of a little girl "who tap-dances for her adoring male relatives ... and grows into a woman who assumes that uncle-shaped men – bulky, balding – are bound to be well-disposed, until just such a colleague at work publishes a spiteful book filled with gossip about the star she has become. This is well judged, and informed by the kind of dismay that a child might feel ..."

Everyone at *Saturday Night* who read the story in manuscript recognized Atwood's source in an instant. Following rigid tradition, she claimed that the character in question had nothing to do with any living person. It was, she said, fiction, as if only silly people would imagine otherwise. That's what she said on *Morningside*, speaking to Peter Gzowski, which in Canadian culture was always the closest thing to being under oath. And – who knows? – it could be the truth. Perhaps all those people who identified me, and perhaps I myself, were projecting our own ideas on to her work. Possibly Shirley Gibson imagined the whole thing. Philip Marchand in *The Toronto Star*, commenting on this issue at the time, noted that people sometimes claim to recognize themselves in significant fiction because they hope it will give them "a form of immortality." Atwood may have had just such a situation in mind when she wrote, in a 1970 poem:

> *In restaurants we argue*
> *over which of us will pay for your funeral*
> *though the real question is*
> *whether or not I will make you immortal.*

This is the function she has been performing, all these years, for Toronto, its topography, and many of its inhabitants. We would be churlish if we were less than grateful.

גמרא (טור מרכזי)

מהו דתימא עקר שליח שליחותיה דבעל הבית
ולא למעל קא משמע לן: **מתני׳**
אמר לו הבא לי מן החלון או מן הדלוסקמא
והביא לו אף על פי שאמר בעל הבית לא היה
בלבי אלא מזה והביא מזה בעל הבית אבל
אם אמר לו הבא לי מן החלון והביא לו מן
הדלוסקמא או מן הדלוסקמא והביא לו מן
החלון השליח מעל שלח ביד חרש שוטה וקטן
אם עשו שליחותו בעל הבית מעל לא עשו
שליחותו החנוני מעל שלח ביד פיקח ונזכר עד
שלא הגיע אצל חנוני חנוני מעל לבשואצא
ביצד יעשה נוטל פרוטה או כלי ויאמר פרוטה
של הקדש בכל מקום שהוא מחולל על זה
שהההקדש נפדה בכסף ובשוה כסף:

גמ׳ מאי קא משמע לן לדברים שבלב
אינם דברים: שלח ביד חרש שוטה וקטן אם
עשו. והא לאו בני שליחותא נינהו אמר רבי
אלעזר עשאום כמעטן של ויתים דתנן הוחיתים
מאימתי מקבלין טומאה משתרועו ויעת המענן
ולא זיעת הקופה הר יוחנן אמר כאותה ששנינו
נתנו על גבי הקוף והולוכו או על גבי חפל
והולוכו ואם ראהר לאהד לקבל ממנו זריזח עירוב
אלמא קא עבדא שליחותיה הכי נמי איתעביד
שליחותיה: שלח ביד פיקח ואף על גב
דלא איירר שליח ורמינהו נוכר בעל הבית ולא
נוכר שליח השליח מעל נוכר שניהם חנוני
מעל אמר רב ששת מתני׳ נמי בשנזכרו שניהן:
מתני׳

Talmudic Thought and the Pleasures of Disputation

Writing about the essays and fiction of the New York Jewish intellectuals in the middle of the twentieth century, Irving Howe said they took intense pleasure in disputation and built their collective style around a sense of tournament, the writer cast as "skilled infighter juggling knives of dialectic." Combat was an essential element in their literary life, and a source of the energy that made the *Partisan Review*, in which they all published, the most compelling intellectual magazine in America – the most loved, the most hated, certainly the most quoted.

More than their radical politics, more even than their didactic urge to introduce current European culture to America, the addiction to conflict distinguished the New York Jewish intellectuals from the relatively genial literary gents who then dominated most of cultural journalism.

In 1976, when I read Howe's comments in his best-seller, *World of Our Fathers* (1976), they lifted my heart. The idea was not new, but Howe's statement of it brought back to me that wonderful moment, in the 1950s, when I discovered the attractions of the tonality shared by Sidney Hook, Clement Greenberg, Irving Kristol, Saul Bellow, and a dozen or so others – including Howe himself, who seemed placid by comparison with some of his colleagues but nevertheless looked (from quiet, earnest Canada) like a ferocious defender of the truth, or at least that small part of the truth he glimpsed.

In those years of my youthful editorial hackery and apprenticeship, I imagined spending some part of my life writing about literature and painting (perhaps other arts as well, eventually), but I saw few models among the gentle, harmless, good-hearted and utterly forgettable critics who populated *The Globe and Mail*, the *New York Times*, and other mainstream publications, even the *Canadian Forum*, for which I wrote from time to time. North American writers on the arts were encouraged to practise the journalism of reassurance. Discussing books or paintings or films, they told their readers that nothing terribly important was happening here, certainly nothing anyone needed to fret about. This writer was "promising," that one was "challenging," but most of what they discussed existed within a narrow band, neither highbrow nor lowbrow but competent and

THE BABYLONIAN TALMUD PUBLISHED BY DANIEL BOMBERG 1519-1523

acceptable – and, in the larger scheme of things, marginal.

A book, Daniel Bell once said, should never satisfy its reader. A book is not a meal. It should make us hungry for writers who will take us deeper into whatever subject it opens for us. The ideal book, if there were such a thing, would be the beginning of a library. In the 1950s every article produced by the New York intellectuals (so it seems in memory) opened possibilities in just that way.

Those warriors of ideology and identity seemed never to achieve, or desire, a sense of completion. They had no ambition to set their subject at rest, which I perceived as the besetting sin of journalistic critics. Whatever they wrote prompted the emergence of further speculations, arguments, shifting truths.

The New York intellectuals were not just outspoken, they were brazen. The toughness and vigour of their arguments applied to every subject, from French existentialism to Eliot's poetry. They had no time for gentility, whereas much of middlebrow journalism had time for little else. Moreover, the New York intellectuals had the learning, originality, and wit to make this hypercritical stance credible, and an urgency in their manner that persuaded readers something important was at stake.

They could, of course, carry this tendency too far. Sometimes, as an editor of mine used to say, they got drunk on the whisky from their own still. Even in far-off Toronto, where exactly one bookstore carried foreign intellectual magazines, a reader could sense that they were straying, consciously or not, into comedy, a self-satire that revealed a certain provincialism.

We are often warned against provincialism, and if we take the warnings seriously we may have trouble figuring out that it's not always a bad thing. In fact, it's usually a crucial part of serious writing. Faulkner is provincial, likewise Borges, Joyce, Davies, Nabokov, Pamuk, Philip Roth, Kundera, and most of the good writers of the world. The most interesting Canadian writer of his generation, Mordecai Richler, was also the most provincial. Each of them speaks to us from a specific locale and would be unrecognizable without it. Isaac Bashevis Singer (whose career was given a burst of life by the *Partisan Review*) put it in four words: "All talent is local."

The many studies of the New York intellectuals have made it clear that, even as they tried to lift themselves above the narrowness of American culture, they created a parish-pump atmosphere all their own. They appear at times to have believed that the most interesting people in the world (the ones they admired and the ones they despised) were members of their own circle, the circle that constantly refreshed itself through their cocktail parties, the 1950s New York equivalent of the literary salon.

This meant they sometimes selected each other as subjects and targets. Leslie A. Fiedler, one of their number, remarked in a 1956 essay that when *Partisan Review* contributors found themselves short of targets they would "gouge and kick each other like marines stirred up to fight among themselves, just to keep their hands in." In novels and stories the same urge came to the surface: "Even the fiction of *PR* tends inevitably toward the roman a clef, its contributors feeding on each other like a mutual benefit association of cannibals."

Studying them taught me to learn through debate – by testing my ideas against the views of others, at first in private and later in public. Argument, I decided, breathes life into facts and history. Argument gives urgency to ideas. It was a quality they possessed and deployed with such power that they passed it on to thousands of people like me. But where did it come from?

It now seems obvious to me that the New York intellectuals were affected in childhood, or family background, or through their friendships, by the Talmudic tradition. Appropriately, the documentary film about Kristol, Bell, Howe, Nathan Glazer, and their generation carries the title *Arguing the World*. Certainly Marxism emphasized debate, but the style was there hundreds of years before Karl Marx was born.

In Jewish texts, controversy is not an event but a habit of mind. Argument is not something that happens now and then, it's the essence of Judaism. It is in the Hebrew Bible, after all, that we meet Job, who quarrelled with God – and even if Job was not a Jew and his story was told originally in a language other than Hebrew, he's a powerful figure who reaches through the Jewish world and far beyond.

The Talmud, that great overflowing fountain of argument, began as conversation in the oral tradition and then was captured in a series of writings that now amount to many volumes. Converting it to words on paper was a response to the harsh new reality of 70 CE, when the Israelites found themselves without a territory or even a temple. Events turned them into a people on the move. Many centuries later Jews would advise each other (sometimes it was a joke; often it wasn't) that one should always keep a bag packed. The Talmud was the most important item in that bag.

Dictionaries call it the embodiment of Jewish civil and ceremonial law, but Jacob Neusner, who has probably written more on this subject than anyone else, calls it a "cookbook of culture composed of recipes for sustaining civilization." It accounts for one of the most striking aspects of Jewish life, its astonishing portability. As Neusner writes in *The Talmud: What It Is and What It Says*, published in 2006, "Wherever Jews have settled and whatever languages they have spoken, they've created a community with a single set of common values. One law, one theology has defined the community throughout their many migrations. A single book explains how this came about: the Talmud."

It was created as a way of explaining the Torah, the Five Books of Moses in the Hebrew Bible, but, as Neusner says, it reframes the Torah "through sustained argument and analysis, encouraging the reader to actively apply reason and logic to his or her thinking."

The place of the Talmud in the thought of Jews, both religious and secular, was illuminated by an argument between two distinguished English writers, Arnold Toynbee (1889-1975) and the Reverend James William Parkes (1896-1981). Five or six decades ago, Toynbee was the most famous historian in the world, far more famous than any historian of today. His fame rested on *A Study of History* (1934), a multi-volume analysis of civilization, in which he developed his general theory of how cultures rise and fall. He affected everyone who thought about human history – including many people who initially considered his work a little dodgy and eventually turned against him.

Toynbee became notorious among Zionists because he considered the establishment of the state of Israel an aberration of history.

He didn't underestimate the ancient Hebrews, and of course, as
a Christian, he saw the Hebrew Bible as the staging platform for
Christianity. But to Toynbee Judaism was not a civilization. Having
been destroyed long ago as a settled human society, it seemed to him
no more than a fossil, the residue of a once living nation. In modern
times its survival seemed pure accident. (Worse, it didn't fit into the
pattern of history he had so carefully constructed.)

Parkes, whose doctoral dissertation at Oxford was entitled *The
Conflict of the Church and the Synagogue: A Study in the Origins of
Antisemitism*, stepped into the argument. Like so many others, he
marvelled at the survival of Judaism during millennia when most of
the other ancient religions and civilizations were reduced to items
in textbooks and exhibits in museums. Parkes thought he knew why.
He believed Judaism remained alive and vital during all those centuries of scattered exile because of the Talmud.

Many Talmudists like to call it an ocean, a vast sea of knowledge,
argument, speculation. Parkes, having spent some time with it, saw
it through Anglican eyes as wildly strange and sometimes incom-
prehensible. He found it an amalgam of laws and pithy sayings but
at the same time a vital part of history, the binding document of
everyday Jewish life, "the moral, recreational and intellectual [food]
of Jews for a millennium."

He knew that Judaism, like Christianity, was challenged by the
Enlightenment. But in the matter of survival the key question faced
by all ancient faiths was not the thought of the eighteenth century
but the harsh reality of the period that began in earnest around 1830.

The nineteenth century brought mass culture, imperialism,
railroads, factories, dynamic new markets, and above all a scientific challenge to religion. Many cultures shrank back in horror. For
Muslims, Mennonites, Buddhists, and a multitude of other communities, the arrival of the nineteenth century was experienced as a
disaster. Old ways of life dissolved, but new ways of life were unac-
ceptable. Certain elements of Orthodox Judaism found themselves
paralyzed by the new world taking shape.

How was it that in this new environment many Jews not only
survived but prospered? By historical accident, the Talmud had

prepared them for seismic change. Parkes explained that, with Talmudic learning behind them, Jews entered the nineteenth century as "not a fossil but a ferment, not a solid phalanx of rigid and unadaptable fundamentalists, but a lively and attractive section of the world's life." He argued that the Jewish Diaspora had been preserved by the Talmud because its voluminous pages functioned as "a root, a unity, an identity, which made it a 'portable homeland.'"

Everywhere they went, the Jews carried versions of the Talmud. And it was the Talmud, as portable homeland, that provided them with intellectual shelter. The Jews persisted, he instructed Toynbee, as a civilization – a civilization largely on paper, but a civilization nevertheless.

Because the scholarship of the rabbis had taught the Jews the intrinsic beauty of disputation, because it had shown them the high value of controversy, they were ready to confront even the most radically changed world. The nineteenth century presented difficult questions, but difficult questions were the daily bread of Jews in the Diaspora.

Arguing the multitude of issues raised in the Talmud, passing on the arguments from generation to generation – that was a central occupation for many of the most talented Jews all over the world. Harold Rosenberg, a brilliant modern art critic and superb polemicist, once wrote that "For 2,000 years the main energies of Jewish communities in various parts of the world have gone into the mass production of intellectuals."

No wonder they were ready for the Industrial Revolution, that rich, dense, disputatious time, with its full-bodied and deeply felt new controversies in everything from politics to biology, from finance to theology. Neusner writes in *Invitation to the Talmud* (1973) that the rabbis who created the Talmud were saintly but not like other saints: "Their sainthood consisted in ... practical and penetrating logic and criticism. Their chief rite was argument. They carried on their religious life and sought sanctity through argument." For them the mind was an instrument of sanctification – not, as so much of the world believes, a way of secularizing every corner of thought and emotion.

The twentieth century was an astonishing period for Jews, the worst and the best since the days of the Temple. In all of Jewish history there's no catastrophe to equal the Holocaust. At the same time, I know of no other period when Jews made such a powerful impression on the world.

Jewish literature flourished in the twentieth century as never before, once we agree that it encompasses books written in Hebrew and Yiddish and goes beyond them into all the languages of the West. Jewish writing created its own capacious multiculturalism. Kafka in German, Osip Mandelstam and Joseph Brodsky in Russian, Primo Levi in Italian, Marcel Proust in French, Ferenc Molnár and Imre Kertész in Hungarian, and of course in English an array of major writers, among them Bellow, Nadine Gordimer, and Roth.

A few Jewish authors, for one reason or another, were baptized. Some had two Jewish parents, some had one. Some had a Jewish education, some did not. But they are defined internationally by an inescapable sense of peoplehood, and the literary quality of that peoplehood comes down to them through the Talmudic tradition. Jewish writers inherit this with their mother's milk; others seek it out. But it's there for everyone who wants it.

The tone of the *Partisan Review* spread through the arts pages and then political discussion. In New York it dominated the *Village Voice* during the late 1950s and early 1960s, when readers learned to expect one *Voice* columnist choosing another *Voice* columnist as the worst example of some squalid cultural trend. You could find it in movie critics, such as Andrew Sarris and the late Pauline Kael, who for a while made a speciality out of not seeing the point of each other's work – and, a few years later, it flowed through the writing of the many film reviewers who followed in their wake. It poked up its head, just a few years later, in all the art critics who defined themselves as pro-Greenberg or anti-Greenberg, and of course in hundreds of book reviewers. Most remarkably, perhaps, it provided the rhetorical foundation for the multitude of neo-conservatives who set a new agenda for American politics by leaning on the beautifully phrased arguments of Irving Kristol, quasi-Trotskyist arguments first honed among the New York intellectuals in their undergraduate days at City College of New York.

Did the writers who played out this historic era in journalism understand that the Talmud haunted their words? Some did, certainly. But many of them were eager to escape the effects of their Jewish education, or the fragments of their parents' Jewish education, or the Jewish style that flavoured the air around them as they grew up. They might not have liked to believe that their way of addressing the world owed a great deal to rabbis in ancient times. Perhaps Leslie Fiedler came closest to accepting this idea when he wrote that among all the immigrant groups who arrived in America in the twentieth century, only the Jews clung to the Old World culture they brought with them, "refusing to cast it into the melting pot with the same abandon with which southern European or Scandinavian peasants were willing to toss away their few scraps of European culture goods." The Talmud, their portable shelter, remained with them – vibrant, infinitely changeable, adaptable to a multitude of uses, but forever passionately, permanently, profoundly argumentative.

Furtive Autobiography:
The Peterborough Journalism
of Robertson Davies

Many things that I would not want to tell anyone, I tell the public;
and for my most secret knowledge and thoughts I send my most
faithful friends to a bookseller's shop. – MICHEL DE MONTAIGNE

On a Dominion Day long ago, CBC radio visited Orillia to collect opinions from people who had once known its most famous citizen, Stephen Leacock. One was a taxi driver who, when asked if he liked Leacock, replied, "No, I don't like him because he didn't like us." Robertson Davies, listening to this, wondered why it was considered necessary for Leacock to like the people of Orillia or anyone else. Perhaps it had to do with Leacock being a humorist, and therefore untrustworthy. Davies took Leacock's side because he loved the man's work and because he considered himself, some part of the time, a humorist.

But the issue doesn't arise only in the context of humour. A close reader of Davies will notice that the question of being liked or not liked played a significant part in the formation of his self-image and his view of the world.

He was at least a part-time journalist all his life, and he wrote an agreeably smooth and occasionally pawky style. For most of his career his journalism was charged with a persistent tension, the conflict between a philistine society and a writer determined to challenge and possibly change it – not always directly, not often with vehemence or anger, but persistently, year by year, as if it were both a duty and a pleasure.

He saw Canada governed by "a cult of genial mediocrity" and wanted something better for his fellow citizens, a larger, more expansive life, culturally and emotionally. In his late novels, beginning with *Fifth Business* (1970), he set this dream in the context of fiction. Earlier, he expressed it in journalism. Why, he wondered, did Canadians settle for so little?

Writing for *Mayfair* magazine in the autumn of 1949, he imagined how his fellow citizens had spent the summer:

> They have rushed about the lakes in noisy little boats....

*they have sat in hot little boats waiting to catch fish which
they have then had to eat.... They have amused themselves after
their fashion and I have no quarrel with them. But their ways are
not my ways, nor are their thoughts my thoughts.*

His apparent tolerance ("I have no quarrel") was more rhetorical
than real. No one was fooled. In truth, he had many quarrels with
the people among whom he spent his life, and he was extremely
conscious of those things that set him apart from them. He had
little time or tolerance for those who did not read – and his acquaintance with many such Canadians did not soften his views. In a
lecture in 1992, three years before his death, he quoted Sir Nathaniel
in *Love's Labour's Lost* on a dullard who knew nothing of books: "His
intellect is not replenished, he is only an animal, only sensible in
the duller parts."

Davies was not an unqualified admirer of democracy. His alter ego,
an invented Davies-like diarist given the name Samuel Marchbanks,
announced at one point his agreement with Théophile Gautier, the
nineteenth-century Romantic poet, who divided "men into two
groups, The Flamboyant and The Drab." Marchbanks/Davies placed
himself firmly among The Flamboyant. "But this is very much the
age of the Drab – the apotheosis of The Squirt. The Squirts and Drabs
are not worth much singly, but when they organize into gangs and
parties they can impose Drabbery and Squirtdom on quite a large
part of mankind."

Comments like that suggest he harboured a certain fear of the
mob. Perhaps that's why, in an age of display, he hid himself with
care. Symbolically, he spent his life in hiding. His beard, while
exuberantly announcing his status as a man of letters, also provided a form of concealment. It was so extravagant that had he shaved
it off he might have been unrecognizable; as a result, most people
who knew him, even over several decades, never caught so much as
a glimpse of his whole face. In retrospect this seems part of a plan.
Davies did disclose his true nature – but slowly, and only to those
who read his work with care.

Lecturing at Yale in 1990, he remarked: "For the greater part of my life the luxury of devoting the best hours of the day to my writing has been denied me. I have always had a job. For twenty-one years I was a journalist, and for much of that time the editor of a daily newspaper."

This was one of the commanding facts of his life. Like Dickens, like Hemingway, like a thousand lesser novelists, Davies was a professional journalist, though working on a daily newspaper was never among the goals the young Davies set for himself. In fact, as a newspaperman he was a conscript.

Davies first came to journalism, as many do, because it seemed an agreeable way to earn a living while using a talent for words. In 1940 he returned from England with his wife, Brenda, to begin a family. He had Oxford behind him, and the Old Vic, where they had both worked under Tyrone Guthrie.

In Toronto, as he recalled late in his life, he first thought of a job on *The Globe and Mail* but discovered it "was going through a mid-life crisis which has existed with it for fifty, sixty, and seventy years." Instead he went to work at B.K. Sandwell's *Saturday Night*, then a slick-paper weekly. He was literary editor as well as second-string drama critic and second-string music critic, his views sometimes appearing under pen-names such as Eleanor Rumming, Margery Maunciple, and Amyas Pilgarlic. This was a genial fraud, more common at the time than today, by which a publication pretended it had a larger staff than was the case. Lucy Van Gogh, the regular drama critic, was in fact Sandwell himself.

Davies liked his job and had no desire, so far as we know, to enter daily journalism and what E.M. Forster called "the world of telegrams and anger." His father, Rupert Davies, an aggressive force in that world, a loyal Liberal elevated to the Canadian senate, needed an editor for the *Peterborough Examiner*, which was the lesser of his two dailies and lived in the shadow of the *Kingston Whig-Standard*. He decided his clever 28-year-old son was the man for the job.

In financial terms, it was a promotion, as Davies realized – but only in financial terms. Otherwise, as Judith Skelton Grant says in *Robertson Davies: Man of Myth* (1978), it felt more like an imposition. It would be hard to identify the charms that a life in Peterborough offered during the Second World War. Moreover, he had no desire to leave Toronto or *Saturday Night*. He had been making a reputation and building a life that was happily some distance from Rupert's dominating personality. In Peterborough he would be just up the road from his father's home in Kingston; and once more he would be put in the adolescent position of having to please his father. His feelings, however, appear to have been irrelevant. It turned out that the offer was no offer at all, more like a command. Rupert Davies, as usual, had his way. In March 1942, Davies became editor of the *Examiner*.

In Peterborough he heard people say, "You know, if you think too much, it will send you crazy." He discovered that Peterborough parents saw education mainly as a means to authenticate their own opinions. Ideally, their children would go off to university and learn that everything they had already heard in Peterborough was true.

Whatever he thought of Peterborough, he took his profession seriously. If he had to be a newspaperman, he would make the best of it. He went at it with will, energy, wit, and considerable success. Soon he was writing some 12,000 words a week for the *Examiner* – editorials, reviews, various items of commentary, and a diary column attributed to the grumpy Marchbanks. When he was editor and then publisher, from the early 1940s to the early 1960s, the *Examiner's* editorials were quoted more often than those of any other paper in the country.

He refused to edit the *Examiner* as a provincial Ontario daily with a circulation of 22,000 just because it happened to be a provincial Ontario daily with a circulation of 22,000. It's clear that he was determined to bring civilization to Peterborough whether Peterborough liked it or not. There was something pathetic in this ambition, and something magnificent as well.

In that regard, he had his triumphs. In the early 1940s Hugh Kenner was an adolescent in Peterborough who had never heard of James Joyce. One day, glancing through the *Examiner*, he came upon a piece about him by Davies. That article arrived at the right time in the right hands. Kenner became an interpreter of modern literature and produced three books about Joyce. While Davies did not make Kenner the wonderfully articulate scholar he became, he helped open him to the possibility of a larger world – roughly the goal of all the journalism Davies produced.

On the other hand, Davies as an editor was capable of obstinate absurdity. In June 1947, the British critic James Agate died. It occurred to Davies that he should write an article saluting this remarkable man, whose work he had often read during his time in England. According to the normal rules of newspapering, the idea of an obituary for Agate in the *Peterborough Examiner* was preposterous. Agate was the drama critic of the *Sunday Times*, the film critic of the *Illustrated London News*, the literary critic of another paper, and a regular on the sort of BBC radio shows where three or four critics would quarrel quietly over the cultural events of the week – some of which, as Agate occasionally confessed later, he never quite got around to attending. He had a taste for Guardsmen and no taste at all for paying his taxes, which made him the centre of both sexual and financial scandals.

Davies ignored those aspects of Agate and wrote of him purely as a drama critic, predicting a great posthumous reputation for him. True, readers of the *Examiner* had never heard of Agate, but Davies predicted their children would hear much of him and their grandchildren even more. There could hardly have been three dozen people in Peterborough who knew that Agate had lived and therefore might be interested to learn that he had ceased to do so. But he was, Davies argued, comparable to Hazlitt, Beerbohm, and Shaw. "The death of Agate means nothing in modern Canada, where the theatre does not flourish; but, as our country assumes the amenities of civilization, his name will mean more and will become in its special sphere a great name."

That was not the most accurate of Davies' prophecies. My guess is that nowadays fewer people in Peterborough know of Agate than in 1947. Still, that wasn't the point. Davies felt like praising a writer who deserved praise. The readers of the *Examiner* could like it or lump it.

He may not have wholeheartedly subscribed to his father's views, but his editorials identified him as a devoted member of the Canadian Establishment. That became clear during a controversy over Vincent Massey's knighthood. In 1954 Prince Philip privately delivered a message from the Queen: Her Majesty wished to confer on her then governor general the Order of the Garter.

The Garter is the greatest gift the Queen can bestow, the highest order of chivalry in England, and the oldest order in the world, having been founded in 1384. Massey would become the first person in the overseas Commonwealth ever to receive it. This was possibly the most ecstatic moment in his life; no upward-striving Anglophile could ask for more.

But, as anyone knows who has read about the career of Lord Black, accepting an honour from the crown is no simple matter for a Canadian. The government did not normally allow Canadians to accept British titles. Massey knew he had to ask Prime Minister Louis St. Laurent's permission. St. Laurent, no Anglophile, delayed a decision as long as he could, until finally he lost the 1957 election and left office. His successor, John Diefenbaker, said he was delighted to hear of Massey's honour but put off for the moment his permission.

Eventually Diefenbaker's chronic procrastination turned into reluctance, and Massey began to despair. He consulted his friend Rob Davies, and Davies came through with an editorial in the *Examiner*.

He argued that, given Massey's great service to crown and country, granting him this favour would be a reasonable exception to an existing policy. He depicted the government's reluctance as an example of narrow-minded Canadianism. Davies asked whether the sovereign was to be allowed to express her gratitude to Massey – "Or are we going to put on our holier-than-thou face and ask her not to smirch the lily whiteness of our egalitarian principles? Could anything be more provincial, more perversely colonial?"

Diefenbaker was not moved, and eventually Massey had to surrender this greatest of all his dreams. The *Examiner* was influential, but not that influential.

For Davies, journalism was a way of exhibiting himself in public. Often, readers could glimpse elements of autobiography elbowing their way into the text. An examination of his book reviews will tell us when his enthusiasm for Sigmund Freud paled and he became instead a devotee of C.G. Jung, who was to have such a profound influence on the novels of his middle age and later. But only the most perceptive reader could have guessed what seems obvious now, that Davies seized on Jung not as an explorer of the psyche but as a source of literary ideas. Davies would treat Jung as Graham Greene treated God; he would draw inspiration from Jung without being governed by him. Jung gave Davies a superstructure for fantasies he was incubating.

In 1961, Davies discussed what he saw as a missed opportunity in J. D. Salinger's *Franny and Zooey*. Most critics thought that Franny's obsessive repeating of a prayer to Jesus was a sign of derangement; we were relieved when her brother somehow talked her out of it and persuaded her that to live properly is prayer enough. Davies, to the contrary, wished Salinger had let Franny keep her obsession; that might have pushed Salinger over into Dostoyevsky country, where something quite interesting could have happened. Was this Davies thinking of his own future? He was then the author of three delightful comic novels about Kingston (thinly disguised as Salterton), but he had – we now know – larger ambitions.

Davies seems to have seen elements of himself in Don Quixote. He wrote that the Don is courteous and chivalrous toward those who use him badly. He's ready to help the distressed or attack tyranny and cruelty. In Davies' view, the Don, mad or not, is "manifestly a greater man than the dull-witted peasants and cruel nobles who torment and despise him." When he mentioned dull-witted peasants, was he thinking of newspaper readers in Peterborough? When he cited cruel nobles, did he think of those who dealt carelessly with his work?

Attending a community theatre production of his play *Fortune, My Foe*, he was startled to hear lines he hadn't written, lines of (as he said) "stupefying vulgarity and foolishness."

The director, it turned out, had changed the script without his approval. The newspaperman in the cast, as Davies had written him, "wasn't stupid enough for a newspaperman," the director said, so the director rewrote the part.

Rather than throttling the man, as some might, or calling his lawyer, as others might, Davies restrained himself. He was playing the game. He had to be a good fellow. After all, how much theatre was there in Canada? How often would his plays be produced?

But an incident of that kind, however sublimated, can never be less than upsetting.

In roughly the same period, Davies finished *Leaven of Malice* and sent it to Clarke Irwin. There it fell under the scrutiny of Irene Clarke, a dragon who breathed fire on all those whose manuscripts displeased her. Mrs Clarke sent back word that she would prefer a happier ending. Davies considered his ending quite happy enough, but (and here the story becomes touching as well as symptomatic) he actually tried to satisfy her desire for what he called an extra half pound of sugar. Twice he sat down to write a new conclusion. Finally he gave up, and so did Mrs Clarke. There must have been times when the phrase "pearls before swine" passed through his mind.

In the early 1960s he wrote for the *Toronto Star* a syndicated column that ran in half a dozen Canadian and American newspapers. It rather annoyed him that the entertainment editor sometimes cut out paragraphs he found displeasing. In any case, Davies withdrew his services after a couple of years. He wrote to a friend: "It pays handsomely, but it is whoredom. To write about... Logan Pearsall Smith for housewives in Sioux Lookout is all right for a while, but in the end it makes one a Tinpot Pontiff." (Smith was the writer who said, "People say that life is the thing, but I prefer reading" – a phrase so attractive to Davies that sometimes he imagined he had invented it.)

Later we find self-evaluations of Davies lurking behind his attitudes to the triumphs and miseries of the celebrated. When Laurence Olivier died in 1989, Davies wrote an obituary for *Maclean's* that sounded like Davies on Davies: "Nobody dared to call him an actor of the old school, but that was precisely what he was and when the old school is the Great Old School it cannot be beaten.... He loved to act, to impersonate... what he liked best were the assumptions of extraordinary personalities."

Despite everything, Davies as a journalist remained charming. But beneath the charm something wondrously passionate was waiting to be unleashed. Those who were watching Davies carefully at the time might have glimpsed it in a paragraph that appeared in the *Toronto Star* about 1960. It concerned Giacomo Casanova. He's often treated as a comic version of Don Juan, but on closer examination he turns out to be a stirring writer, a soldier, a scholar, a musician, and a crook who knew precisely what he was doing and watched himself with an amused eye. The thought of Casanova brought back to Davies something said by the headmaster of Upper Canada College, W. L. Grant, when Davies was a student there. One Sunday evening Dr Grant startled an audience of schoolboys by shouting "Live dangerously; sin nobly!"

Casanova, Davies wrote in the *Star*, had certainly done that. But the boy Davies must have wondered if he could ever follow advice so outrageous. Could he develop an imagination that was grand, dangerous, and in traditional Canadian terms sinful? He took many years to find the answer, but in the end it was a triumphant Yes.

In the Theatre of Memory

He kept a journal, Charles Ritchie said, because he didn't want life to slip away from him like sand slipping through his fingers. He was right not to trust memory as the keeper of his past. Fortunately, he was foresighted enough to write a clear, often funny, sometimes remorseful account of his superb career as a Canadian diplomat and his exciting private life as, among other things, the lover for several decades of the Anglo-Irish novelist Elizabeth Bowen. After retiring from the public service Ritchie became a much-admired man of letters when his journals appeared as a series of books, most notably *The Siren Years*, winner in 1974 of a Governor General's Award.

Dead since 1995, he still shows up in bookstores as the co-star of *Love's Civil War* (2009), the searching, serious, and profoundly gossipy book that Victoria Glendinning has made from his diaries and Bowen's letters. Ritchie defeated the forgetfulness that destroys most of the past and determined that we would remember him on his own terms. To a modest but satisfying degree, he imposed himself on history. He passed on to thousands of readers his views of everything he cared about, from the quality of John F. Kennedy's administration (mediocre, he thought) to the torments of a sensitive intellectual's yearning for love. He knew how to deal with the most devious of our faculties: He was a virtuoso of memory management.

Human memory is a marvellous but fallacious instrument, Primo Levi wrote. He lived a tragic life he was desperate to recount, of survival in a Nazi death camp. His narrative ability was so developed that he became one of the world's great witnesses of that crime. Still, he cautioned us to treat recollection with care: "The memories which lie within us are not carved in stone." They change as time passes and may increase by incorporating "extraneous features." He understood, after working with his own memory for decades, that even honest people adjust, edit, and sometimes fundamentally revise their memories – usually without knowing what they are doing, sometimes to the consternation or amusement of friends who were present in the same place at the same time and know it wasn't like that at all.

Once observed and noted by the mind, the past becomes subject to every conceivable form of distortion and amplification. Memory's favourite pastime is unauthorized improvisation. "Oral history," a form of narrative that grew popular in the 1960s and was often advertised as a way to study the lives of working-class people and others who have traditionally been neglected by historians, continues to be regarded with suspicion by academics; they know all too well that memory is the historian's most subtle opponent.

Once an old colleague and I discussed frankly the long-ago suicide of his brother-in-law, a distinguished and remarkable man whose family kept the cause of his death secret for decades. Three or four years after that first conversation, my colleague and I met again and the same death came up. But now he said in passing, assuming I would agree, that his brother-in-law had died of a heart attack, as the newspaper obituaries falsely claimed; certain people had guessed it was a suicide, he said, but they were wrong. For some reason his memory had rewritten a crucial scene from his life – or perhaps he had decided it was best after all, for history's sake, to re-adopt the false story. In that case his memory had erased our previous meeting. I had been otherwise in touch with the family, but I let his revised version pass without comment. It seemed too delicate a matter to dispute.

We often hear people praised for having good memories, and we often hear others complain that they can never remember faces or names or something else they would like to retrieve. We usually know what they mean, though without necessarily understanding that the word "memory" changes from one era to another. People early in the last century were praised for having a good memory if they could declaim at will a small library of poetry. Today a good memory means being able to recall sports statistics or obscure cultural trivia.

Memory's status among human talents is in fact just as unstable as memory itself. In the last half of the twentieth century most educational systems in the West gave up the idea that memorizing was an essential part of learning. "Memory work," once the duty of all school-children, fell out of favour; "rote learning" became a term of disapprobation. In recent years it's been a rare school that has required students to recite poetry "by heart." Educators decided instead to emphasize creative thinking rather than the accumulation of data. Much anecdotal evidence suggests that they were so anxious to demote the practice of memory work that they began to turn out students who were essentially ignorant about not only history, public affairs, and culture but also the data necessary to make their way in the world.

In this context the belief in the value of memory that was held for a good many centuries now seems quaint. And yet many of the thinkers who held that belief (Aristotle, for instance, or St. Thomas Aquinas) remain touchstones in the philosophy of the West. We study what they memorized but resolutely refuse to memorize it.

In Europe during the Medieval and Renaissance periods, a man hoping to be thought wise couldn't do better than present evidence of a spectacular memory. Scholars would give public displays of their learning, some of them boasting of their ability to quote in Latin or Greek all of the important classical authors. Debaters thought nothing of spontaneously inserting in their arguments direct quotations running thousands of words long.

They usually depended on a mnemonic device known variously as the Method of Loci, Memory Theatre, or Memory Palace. The technique was developed in antiquity, was mentioned by Aristotle and Cicero, and was revived in the monasteries of Europe.

A scholar would choose a building he knew well, or mentally construct an imaginary building. He would imagine each room fitted out with furniture and other objects that symbolized ideas or material to be quoted. Memorizing a speech or a work of literature, the speaker would first separate it into sections, then decide on the location for each piece. While speaking he would move mentally through the rooms of his building, picking up facts where necessary. He would know the imaginary building and its contents so well that he could slip into any corner of it at will, even work from the last room back through to the first. The theory, proven by generations of scholars, was that visually recalling spaces and objects triggers memory. A building, in particular, has a coherence and logic that mnemonically connects one thought or fact with another.

One famous scholar, Giulio Camillo (1480-1544), developed this idea in a spectacularly literal way: he believed it would work even better if a speaker, when gazing out at an audience, could see figures and ornaments suggesting his text, painted on pillars. He set out to construct a wooden Memory Theatre and wrote a book about it, *L'idea del Theatro* (1550). Camillo never completed his invention but showed it in rough form in Venice and Paris, becoming in the process the talk of scholarly Europe.

Alas, nothing but the book survives. But the same system operates today in the work of performers like Dominic O'Brien, a British mnemonist who has won the world memory championship eight times and written books about his technique, among them *How to Develop a Perfect Memory* (1993) and *Quantum Memory Power* (2001). He calls his equivalent of the Memory Theatre system a "journey" and, just like Renaissance scholars, translates all his facts and numbers into memorable images. He and a few others, performing astounding memory tricks in public, are the survivors of a tradition that was once a crucial part of intellectual life.

Sue Halpern, in her recent book about memory research, *Can't Remember What I Forgot* (2009), makes the point that memory "is not an archive." It exists within the human brain in the form of "chemical traces" which fade and can be augmented. It resides not in one place but throughout the brain.

The life we lead after any given event may well cause us to reshape our inner record of it, so that it fits within a coherent pattern. In the only sense that our brain contains an archive, it's a surrealistic version of a library in which squads of anonymous gnomes patrol the shelves, stealing some files, rewriting others. Medical researchers have proven that the brain is far more malleable than was known even twenty years ago, as Norman Doidge demonstrated in his recent book, *The Brain That Changes Itself* (2007). Perhaps they will eventually discover that memory is the most compliant, yielding, and therefore untruthful part of our mental equipment. Hume Cronyn, the distinguished actor, called his autobiography *A Terrible Liar: A Memoir* (1991), explaining in the foreword that "memory can be a terrible liar."

The past is a theatre where the mind reworks fragments of incident into a narrative that we call the self. Memory constantly re-stages itself like a playwright reworking an unsatisfactory script. Perhaps it presents the past in the form that will be most comfortable to us when we recall it. Or it may organize itself so as to meet our literary standards as storytellers. However it works, this process forces us to live on the basis of information that is at best shaky. When we consider that fact, our admiration for a careful diarist like Ritchie grows.

With all its faults, memory remains the key to identity. We exist as individuals because we remember that we did this and not that, loved these people but not those, believed certain things and dismissed others. Emotionally and intellectually we are no more than our accretion of memory. What we call "memory" and what we call "consciousness" are almost identical.

The importance of memory is brought to our attention most forcefully, and tragically, when we encounter or read about an Alzheimer's victim. Those who lose memory through Alzheimer's sooner or later are annihilated as individuals with unique identity.

Of all the nightmares George Orwell explored in *Nineteen Eighty-Four*, the one that most powerfully resonates with us today is the memory hole. His protagonist Winston lives under a dictatorship that seeks to cleanse humanity of treasonous memories by banishing all evidence of them. Citizens are taught to dispose of documents and other proof of past events through a sewer: "When one knew that any document was due for destruction, or even when one saw a scrap of waste paper lying about, it was an automatic action to lift the flap of the nearest memory hole and drop it in, whereupon it would be whirled away on a current of warm air to the enormous furnaces which were hidden somewhere in the recesses of the building."

In 1948, when he was writing that dystopian classic, Orwell had in mind various practices developed in the Soviet Union, such as the hiding of embarrassing court records and the alteration of photographs to erase the images of political leaders who had angered Stalin. That's no doubt how *Nineteen Eighty-Four* moved people when it appeared.

The fall of the Soviets did not banish from the earth the political
habit of lying about the past (the Russian government has recently
been trying to improve even Stalin's reputation), but anyone reading about the memory hole in the twenty-first century will more
likely think about our steadily intensifying fear of Alzheimer's.
Improved diet and improved medicine have brought increased
longevity to much of the world, a great benefit with an unhappy
side effect; many who would have died sooner now live long enough
to endure a wretched Alzheimer's death caused by the potential
memory hole that may well be living, undetected, within us. For a
mind that still works, memory provides fantasy, terror, and satisfaction as well as identity. But when Alzheimer's strikes, the absence
of memory becomes the ultimate tragedy for a living human, the
obliteration of being.

A Box Full of History: TV and Our Sense of the Past

On television one recent evening Buddy Rich (1917-1987) was playing a solo as the other musicians in his band sat in patient silence, watching the master work. A drum solo can be mind-numbing, a senseless demonstration of ego and physical strength that quickly exhausts the patience of the audience. Or it can be, in the hands of a virtuoso like Rich, four or five minutes of ecstatic concentration, a sweet abandonment of self, a noisy cousin of Zen meditation.

The good drum solo stands outside the normal boundaries of music in a place all its own, beyond tonality, a separate realm of rhythm and sound dynamics. It abandons notes, chords, and melodies in favour of a structure that the drummer designs spontaneously, inventing his own logic and creating his own momentum as he goes. The great drummers ignore the audience when working, losing themselves in the ingenious deployment of their muscles as they rush down the baroque corridors of their own architecture. But even as the drummer forgets us we realize that this event contains powerful elements of the visual. Who can watch it without enjoying the look of the equipment that the musician coaxes to life? Who can ignore the light that dances off the Zildjian cymbals or the exuberant chromium on the rims of the drums? The Cubist complexities of the drum set, with its primitive lever-and-gear technology, slowly reveal themselves under the scrutiny of the camera, making a drum solo perfect television.

Intensity rises and falls as the performer drives us through climaxes and anticlimaxes, great thunderous bursts alternated with feathery passages so delicate that they walk up to the very edge of silence before coming back to us. The drum solo, when it works, amounts to a one-player drama that subsumes all the performer's talents in a single wordless narrative, emerging as exquisite theatre.

All of this Buddy Rich, dead now for 18 years, delivered to my bedroom, unannounced as usual. Pushing the buttons on my remote-control wand, I stumbled on the solo just as it began. Where was this tape made? When? As so often happens, television did not tell me. The musician's clothes suggested it was around 1980, when

Rich was in his sixties, still working, a marvel of energy and survival in a profession that killed many before their time.

Television didn't pause to celebrate this miracle and didn't seem interested in the fact that it was showing us a piece of cultural history. In truth, it seems possible that the people who run television are a little ashamed of the old tapes and films they replay, as if anything less than new carried a stigma. They haven't yet developed a sub-profession of broadcasting scholars to explain the date, provenance, and context of whatever appears on the screen. The television people are unaware that a great museum of history has fallen into their hands. It will be some time before they understand the opportunities and duties this inheritance brings with it.

A sense of the past has become one of the great gifts of television, and one for which I grow steadily more grateful. Only 20 years ago it was commonplace to argue that television was creating a present-tense society in which memory lost meaning. No one could say that now. A multitude of channels, rerunning the triumphs and disasters of the past, provides viewers of the early twenty-first century with a visual history that was available to no previous generation.

History is always with us on television: soldiers storming the beaches of Normandy, the caisson carrying John Kennedy's body to Arlington, the student defying the tank in Tiananmen Square, the Berliners turning their hated wall into fragments for sale to tourists, O.J. Simpson getting away with murder before our eyes. Television displays, perhaps with even more effectiveness, another kind of history, the texture of life as lived 50 or 60 years ago. It plucks out of the past all the details no one thought important at the time, details we now view with the fascination of amateur anthropologists.

Once upon a time, public events possessed a grave formality: congressional hearings, plays, and office work all required that men show up in jackets and ties; a law, apparently, decreed that men on the street must wear fedoras at all times. Houses in situation comedies were all designed in the same style, more or less up-to-date and certainly with huge windows. In that distant era many of the most beautiful women were heavy by twenty-first century standards, their faces heavily made up.

Television delivers a third kind of history with even more effectiveness, the history of itself. As it grows older and the channels grow more numerous, television turns increasingly to its vaults. This means that I can turn on television at an odd moment, perhaps while getting dressed in the morning, and find myself transfixed by a black and white production of *The Cocktail Party*, by T.S. Eliot, a now-forgotten play that was once taken seriously as a Christian exploration of contemporary sensibility. As the work of a mid-century intellectual, it naturally deals with both psychiatry and martyrdom.

This production is from 1960, which means there was no videotape yet. We watch a kinescope, an always murky kind of early recording. We find the CBC drama department at its most self-conscious and serious, when it believed its duty was to display the "important" plays of the era before a mass audience. It might have been tedious when it first appeared; now it has the patina and charm of age. It speaks more of anglophile Canada 45 years ago than of Christianity or even Eliot; there are seven principal actors, each of them bearing a name from the British Isles. The late Jane Mallett is in the cast, her mannered performance rendered historic rather than annoying. The youngish-looking man is William Hutt, 40 years old. He's not yet Canada's favourite Lear or Tartuffe. He's sharp and sardonic in his self-absorbed way.

Moments like this give entertainment a stimulating dimension of time. We can now see television in layers, noting differences in performance, content, and above all pacing (everything was much slower then, from the commercials to the movement of cameras and the editing). The situation of television has slowly come to resemble the context in which we understand printed material; we can begin to compare one era's ideas with another, laugh at or respect our ancestors as we reinterpret what they believed according to our own knowledge and sensibility. Our understanding of the people we watch naturally colours our responses. When Judy Garland sang "The Battle Hymn of the Republic" on her program the week after John F. Kennedy's murder, she looked grave and resolute. Today, watching the same performance, knowing that she died just six years later, we may see little but her fragility, her wan attempt to hide desperation behind the courage that the moment required.

For those who want it, this kind of experience grows more available with every season, on channels like Bravo, History, BookTelevision, the Documentary Channel, CoolTV, the Independent Film Channel, and the multitude of channels devoted to old films. Elsewhere ancient TV series reappear, from *I Love Lucy* to *The Rockford Files*, displaying tastes and habits that the old have mostly forgotten and the young never knew.

Lately I've discovered a British series called *Playing Shakespeare*, in which John Barton of the Royal Shakespeare Company works through a few scenes with half a dozen actors. Together they unlock a text, discovering what words and phrases to stress, where to breathe, what meaning Shakespeare encoded in the words, how the actors should react to each other. Barton comes across as a master teacher and a bit of a TV star (like Buddy Rich, he forgets the camera). What makes this historic is that the lessons take place in 1982 and the actors he works with – Ben Kingsley, Judi Dench, Ian McKellan – are among the best of their generation, all caught relatively early in their distinguished careers. It offers a privileged glimpse of a long-ago reality.

Ancient public affairs programs have a similar effect. In the 1950s and 1960s Nathan Cohen chaired *Fighting Words*, a kind of intellectual argument that appeared on the CBC late on Sunday afternoon, bringing with it an astonishing parade of artists and heavy thinkers, from Morley Callaghan to Hannah Arendt to Isaiah Berlin. These programs, showing up now on BookTelevision, provide delightful (sometimes) glimpses of what Canadians thought was important two generations ago. Occasionally I have even come upon my young self pontificating for the *Fighting Words* audience on some now antique topic. To my horror, I once saw myself pause self-importantly, in mid-oration, to light a cigarette. Well, I was young. So was television.

In 1950 the radio critic of the London *Daily Mail* (a newspaper never considered a world-beater) wrote that "Television is the biggest time-waster ever invented.... People will sit watching for hours – even when they don't care much for the programmes they're viewing.... It's so easy to sink into an armchair and switch on entertainment until bedtime." He wanted a royal commission set up to investigate the "hypnotic effect." Poor man, he had no idea of the horrors to come. At that moment there was only one channel in England, operated by the BBC.

In the spring of 1961, Newton Minow, a previously little-known lawyer, became a celebrity by denouncing American television. As Kennedy's newly appointed chairman of the Federal Communications Commission, he was addressing a convention of the National Association of Broadcasters. He told them that when television is good it's powerful and eloquent, "But when television is bad, nothing is worse. I invite you to sit down in front of your television set when your station goes on the air and .... keep your eyes glued to that set until the station signs off." The fact that no one uses television this way didn't discourage him. He believed he had articulated an important point. He told the broadcasters they would see a procession of game shows, violence, audience participation shows, formula comedies about totally unbelievable families, more violence, etc.

"I can assure you that you will observe a vast wasteland." That phrase went into the dictionaries of quotations and in later years achieved even more eminence by becoming the basis of questions on Jeopardy!, Trivial Pursuit, and Who Wants to Be a Millionaire? For years no one spoke of TV without using the word "wasteland." Minow set the tone for respectable attitudes to television. He made it acceptable for just about anyone to look down on it. The intellectually stunted, the emotionally dead, the culturally blind: they can all take a superior position when giving their views on television.

To this day, newspaper columnists who may not have had a fresh thought in decades nevertheless feel licensed to tell us that TV is worthless. They know we would be astonished if they told us anything else. Those who write regularly about television are unique among critics, being the only reviewers assigned to analyze what they find inherently despicable. They believe themselves severely put upon, and they make their readers (not to mention the broadcasters) suffer for the pain and indignity they must endure while watching programs beneath their contempt.

In order to maintain this stance, one must ignore much of television and concentrate only on current programs, if possible the worst of those – the "reality" shows are a mine of inspiration for those seeking the pleasures of chronic disapproval. Meanwhile, many of us are looking elsewhere, happily exploring the history that television so generously provides.

The most interesting moments retrieved from the past are often the result of happy accidents, the work of unsung heroes in archives departments who had the sense to keep the kinescopes or videotapes in a safe place until someone recognized their value. This is not, of course, the history that television celebrates. Pious television executives and bureaucrats like to lecture us on history as something we are compelled, out of duty, to absorb in its quasi-official form. What they admire, and vigorously sell, are programs that in structure parallel the books they studied in school – programs that select some choice theme for examination and then deliver it coherently to the audience, if possible with an actual book published as a tie-in.

In their lectures on the significance of whatever self-conscious history programs they have just made, TV people like to quote George Santayana's "Those who cannot remember the past are condemned to repeat it," possibly the most fatuous of all contemporary mantras. Teachers, journalists, and textbook publishers use Santayana to intimidate those who are not yet impressed by the Federalist Papers or the BNA Act. But anyone who thinks about it for a moment will see the flaw in Santayana's claim. Some of the great figures of recent times, such as Winston Churchill and Harry Truman, were devoted students of history, yet they were condemned to repeat the disasters of war, though of course with variations. Surely there was never a generation more learned in history than the young men who graduated from Oxford and Cambridge in the early years of the twentieth century; and they went off to die needlessly and (some would say) thoughtlessly in the trenches of the First World War.

Yet we persist in arguing for history on instrumental grounds, as if it will help us avoid future peril. Governments and public broadcasters have other demands to make on it; they expect history to buttress national spirit, justify our system of government, fill us with something like civic pride. This impulse leads to a demagogic assertion that Canada's history is, as many popular historians argue, "just as exciting and interesting as anyone else's," which would be an invitation to ribald laughter if Canadians had not silently agreed to hear all such nonsense with solemn faces. That argument is usually made by someone trying to sell a book, justify a TV budget, or set up a new curriculum. In no other circumstances would it be possible to suggest that a history that lacks a Napoleon or a Lincoln or a Churchill is just as interesting as a history that possesses such figures.

The national and educational arguments for history as a source of social improvement are made during the promotion of programs such as *The Civil War*, the 1990 series Ken Burns made for Public Television in the US, or *Canada: A People's History*, which Mark Starowicz produced five years ago for the CBC. These can be good programs, but they have the disadvantage of embodying a past that's been processed by professors and broadcasters. *Canada: A People's History*, for all its virtues, teaches us that from the beginning Canada has been a land of conned and defeated populations, a sea-to-sea convention of losers: natives victimized by whites, French victimized by British, Scots victimized by English (who drove them out of Scotland), and of course everyone victimized by the Americans. As the list of the oppressed grows, from program to program, a viewer may wonder how it happened that these wretched and demoralized people ended up owning a country rich enough to pay for *Canada: A People's History*.

That approach to our history no doubt deserves airing, but the CBC distributes it without any indication of its flaws, as the only ambitious account of our past delivered by our broadcasters in this generation. I would not like to have missed it; but as I watched it I realized that almost every incident it portrays could have been shown from an entirely different perspective, or perhaps several different perspectives. This is the problem that never fails to arise with big-budget network history in the manner of Burns or Starowicz.

Another kind of history, unmediated and unpromoted, freed from committees and consultants, reaches us in the spaces between significant programming. It comes to us routinely and offhandedly, in romances that are at least half true to their period, in TV serials that try to create period tone (like *Little House on the Prairie* or *Anne of Green Gables*), in war stories that at least suggest the nature of military life.

Santayana had it wrong when he suggested history could help us frame our future. Knowing it probably won't help us avoid the calamities to come and may not even make us any wiser. Nevertheless, it remains essential. History thickens daily existence and gives life meaning by linking us with chains of ancestors. History, if understood even a little, becomes the background against which we enact our lives. Without some personal sense of history, we work on an empty stage. Television, these days, helps fill that stage with a magnificent array of props.

Deceit, Parody, and the Furtive Pleasures of Art

The legend of Nat Tate was tragic, but it evoked hopeful memories of Van Gogh, whose early death and later resurrection became the model for what the art world considers a tragedy with a happy ending: a miserable life followed eventually by gigantic auction prices.

In Greenwich Village in the 1950s Tate painted in the Abstract Expressionist mode. He was friendly with his famous contemporaries and apparently accepted by them. He had the requisite affair with Peggy Guggenheim, who treated the New York painters roughly the way Catherine the Great handled the Russian officer corps. Tate seemed be on the way to success, at the side of Pollock, Rothko, and the rest.

But the early interest in his work soon faded and along with it his confidence. He examined his paintings and judged them inadequate. In despair, he decided he would no longer burden the world with his presence. He burned most of his pictures and took a one-way trip on the Staten Island Ferry. His body was never recovered.

His story came to light in a handsome 1998 book by William Boyd, the English novelist: *Nat Tate – An American Artist: 1928-1960*. It included reproductions of the few surviving Tate works and carried on the cover an appreciative blurb by Gore Vidal. It was launched in a fashionable New York gallery, where David Bowie read excerpts from the text and John Richardson, Picasso's biographer, gave a talk about Tate's meetings with Picasso and Braque.

It soon developed that all of this was an elaborate work of fiction. There was no Nat Tate. The appearances of Bowie and Richardson were real, but they were there to play roles in an amiable game. Boyd, who was at the time on the board of *Modern Painting* magazine, dreamt up Nat Tate, executed his paintings, and plucked anonymous photographs from junk shops to serve as pictures of the artist.

This was both a hoax and a parody, two forms that intersect and can often be confused. It was a *jeu d'esprit*, like many hoaxes, but it was also a parody of art journalism. The artist's name was borrowed from two London museums, the National Gallery and the Tate; his biography was borrowed from the vast accretion of feature-story mythologies that gather around the making of art.

There are simple jokes, and there are serious jokes. When an artist consciously puts together the two elements that Freud defined as the main characteristics of jokes, displacement and surprise, provocative questions are raised.

Writers and painters often throw themselves into this form of play in order to shed their normal solemnity and reveal vagrant quirks of personality. Typically, artists start their careers in the earnest hope that they and their work will be taken seriously by the public. But when acclaim finally arrives it's often hard to handle. They find themselves drafted into the uncomfortable ranks of sages, expected to speak regularly and wisely on all manner of serious subjects.

In a mild form of hoaxing, Graham Greene found his own way of resisting this fate. Whenever a London literary magazine challenged its readers to devise parodies of distinguished writers, Greene would submit a dead-on self-parody under a pseudonym and claim the prize.

Play of that kind reflects the humanity of artists and celebrates their autonomy. It's a knowing sideways glance at the audience, a furtively shared form of comic self-disclosure.

Nat Tate's non-existence was soon revealed. An English journalist, attending the book launch, found it curious that he met no one who claimed to have known Tate but, also, no one who admitted that the name was new to them. Karen Wright, who as editor of *Modern Painters* was among Boyd's co-conspirators, was amused to find people saying "Yes, I've heard of him." No one disputed that Tate's death was a melancholy event for art. No one wanted to appear uninformed.

Boyd was astonished at the way Tate's non-life developed. He kept expecting it to fade away, but it never has. Over ten years his hoax became the subject of three television documentaries in Britain. Boyd was cast as an expert on hoaxes and was asked to comment every time a new one became known. He heard from PhD students who wanted permission to quote Nat in their theses. He received letters from people who claimed to be Nat Tate. In November 2010 Boyd found himself on stage in a Berlin art gallery, talking about Nat for an audience of several hundred. Nat's alleged face, magnified many times, looked down from the wall.

Eventually Boyd "found" (that is, created) another recovered Tate drawing. He had it elegantly framed and took it to Sotheby's. It was accepted for the Modern & Post-War British Art sale, the proceeds to be donated to the Artists' General Benevolent Institution, founded in 1814 by J.M.W. Turner. At the auction in November 2011, bidding was brisk and quickly passed the top estimate of 5,000 [pounds sterling]. It sold for 7,250 [pounds sterling]. It was not established whether the anonymous collector was an admirer of Tate or Boyd or both. At the end there was a sense that the world had not heard the last of Nat Tate.

There's nothing mythical about Brian Jungen, a Canadian artist born in British Columbia in 1970, of Swiss and Dunne-za First Nation ancestry – except, of course, his subjects. He's the most striking parodist in Canadian art, and most of his parodies involve mixing mythic native imagery with modern manufacturing.

His inspiration goes as far back as Giuseppe Arcimboldo (1527-1593), the clown prince of Renaissance artists. Arcimboldo's artistic presence rested on metamorphosis, and so does Jungen's. The twenty or so Arcimboldo paintings known to art history are portraits in which the faces of the subjects are formed from vegetables, fruit, and every imaginable kind of seafood. The results are grotesque but also arresting and memorable. The produce is painted with exquisite care but shaped into the unlikely form of human heads. This art of displacement has won Arcimboldo a place in the museums and art books of the world, and a loyal public. What he offers is not just a brilliant curiosity or a visual joke; he also unsettles our perceptions, casually introducing us to the idea that radically different objects (a shrimp and a human nose, for instance) are not so unlike each other as we might have thought. Arcimboldo was a surrealist long before the word was invented.

Brian Jungen, the child of a technological era, chooses, as building blocks of his work, not vegetables or fish but slickly designed consumer products. In Jungen's hands golf bags mutate into totem poles, and a cluster of white plastic garden chairs is reborn as the skeleton of a whale.

He doesn't hide the origins of these consumer products. In fact, their continuing visibility as what they were in the beginning is essential to the joke, just as with Arcimboldo. The lawn chairs do not cease to be lawn chairs even though they have been transmuted into a convincing whale skeleton or a prehistoric fish. He celebrates the triumph of imagination over material fact, the magic way it hints that a few nudges from an artist can upset the reality of mundane life.

On a more subtle level he depicts native culture's ability to borrow the results of Western design and redeploy them as flesh versions of tradition. On this level there's an element of melancholy mixed with the comic and the satiric. Paul Chaat Smith, a Comanche and the associate curator of the National Museum of the American Indian in Washington, has said that Jungen is "that rare artist whose work is accessible yet unsettling, funny yet infused with loss."

One day, over 60 years ago, I caught my first and still favourite example of sly, impish deceit in autobiography. The author was Vladimir Nabokov, perhaps the most playful of all great artists of the twentieth century. I was reading with intense pleasure *Speak, Memory* (1951), his enthralling memoir reaching from his infancy in Russia through his wandering émigré years in Europe to his arrival in America in 1940.

At the end I was introduced (with the help of a hint from a more knowledgeable friend) to the Nabokovian version of clandestine comedy. Describing exiled Russian writers he knew in western Europe, he said that the one who most interested him was Sirin, a member of his own generation. "He was the loneliest and the most arrogant." Beginning with his first novel in 1925 "until he vanished as strangely as he had come," Sirin was criticized for offending the Russian sense of decorum. Critics took a morbid pleasure in finding him disturbing. "He passed like a meteor," leaving not much behind him except "a vague sense of uneasiness."

As my friend told me, this was Nabokov's comment on himself. He published some of his first books in Russian under the pen name V. Sirin – novels I was later to know well as a reviewer when he produced English versions in the 1960s. Aside from sharing a joke with readers who knew this fact (not many did in 1951), this was his way of setting the American Nabokov apart from the European Nabokov, shedding his skin. He was also thickening the sense of mystery surrounding his works. And there was no doubt an element of truth in his self-assessment, which he chose to present in the third person.

Beyond that, Nabokov was introducing to his readers the silliness that was a crucial part of his makeup. We who were to read him over the decades that followed eventually learned that he wanted us to be aware of this element in his character. He was not interested in playing the Great Man venerated by his admirers. In his letters he was careful to present his buoyant side through word play. He loved Proust but noted that his name "anagrimes" (Nabokov's verb meaning "changes into") "stupor," a hint of his condition when the past floated back to him. He disliked T.S. Eliot and anagrimed him as "toilets." He made himself a minor character, "Vivian Darkbloom" (an anagram of "Vladimir Nabokov"), in *Lolita* and *Ada, or Ardor*.

In his collection *Lectures on Literature* (1980), we find him including in his discussion of *Mansfield Park* the fact that Jane Austen set it in 1807, the same year Thomas Jefferson signed the Embargo Act regulating British shipping. Then he adds, "If you read embargo backwards, you get 'O grab me.'" That wasn't Nabokov's discovery; enemies of Jefferson gave it that name and in fact imagined a squirrel-sized animal, the Ograbme, which was said to harass legitimate American shippers, nipping at their ankles. Nabokov must have come upon this in his study of American history and decided it was just the detail that would bring a lecture to life by changing the mood of the classroom.

The book Nabokov left unfinished at his death, *The Original of Laura*, has a character, an old novelist, who tries to eliminate himself with his rubber eraser, beginning with his toes and moving upward. It's possible that Nabokov, no great lover of literary theory, was concocting his answer to the famous 1967 essay by Roland Barthes, "The Death of the Author." Or perhaps he had in mind the inventions of America's greatest graphic artist, Saul Steinberg, who specialized in visual/literary trickery, including artists vanishing from the page by their own hands.

When it comes to arcane literary mysteries it's impossible to ignore the King James Bible. I don't mean the theological inconsistencies. I'm referring to the problem of Psalm 46, a great Psalm indeed ("God is our refuge and strength") but the source of a not terribly important though definitely insoluble conundrum.

It was mentioned in December 2011 in the *Times Literary Supplement* by Stephen Prickett, Regius professor emeritus of English at the University of Glasgow and editor of the *Oxford World's Classics Bible*. As he notes, if we take the forty-sixth word from the beginning and the forty-sixth word from the end and combine them, we get "shake-spear." Add to this that Shakespeare was 46 in 1611 when the book came out, and throw in the fact that he was born on April 23, half of 46.

"We surely have a choice worth pondering," Prickett wrote, "between improbable chance and equally improbable design." If it seems unlikely anyone would have gone to the trouble of arranging that sequence of words, it also seems improbable that it happened by accident.

A letter to the editor of the TLS criticized Prickett for succumbing to this "hoary old myth." It is indeed old, and at the moment you can find discussions of it at 187,000 sites on the Web. It appears sometimes in popular literature, as in Neil Gaiman's graphic novel, *Sandman*, where Shakespeare shows up and explains the whole business: "They gave me some of the psalms to prettify. Ah, vanity, vanity. I hid my name in a psalm."

It seems unlikely that Shakespeare had time for this sort of thing. Still, if we choose to think that someone did it on purpose we should consider the possibility mentioned by Prickett. Facetiously, he writes: "My candidate would be James I: the only man with both a taste for the theatre, and the power to make last-minute alterations to the text. But who knows?" It's an attractive idea, at least, that this whole parade of literary deceit, trickery, and mystification was set in motion by the same royal personage who left us our great translation of the Bible. Even Nabokov would approve.

"Mike's story becomes unstuck when h[e] yields to the call of narcolepsy, to th[e] oneiric, to a secondary dream-state with[in] in the already-acknowledged dream[-] state of film, a move that renounces th[e] search for hermeneutic templates tha[t] might measure characters' achievemen[t] of autonomy, subjectivity, or integrity o[r] the extent of a film's deviation from ge[-] neric or ideological norms. For film criti[-] cism to become oneiric in this sense woul[d] mean to replace hermeneutic studies wit[h] acts of letting-go or creative drift ..."

These are sentences that beg to be pu[t] out of their misery, yet they come from the word processor of an English pro[-] fessor. In that regard they are not unusu[-] al. We can now expect to encounter ac[-] ademics who have spent years reading Shakespeare or Jane Austen yet proud[-] ly turn out barbarous prose and en[-] courage young people to imitate them.

Slumberous Mumblement in Academe: Tortured Sentences, Strangled Thoughts

They live in their own private Utopia, Theorylandia, an imaginary country where there are many printing presses but no editors, and all the citizens are professors or graduate students. Verbs are the staple crop. In cottage workshops the people spend their days processing verbs, preparing the product for packaging and export.

They problematize issues, totalize generalizations, mediate identities, historicize social customs, refuse absolutely to privilege meta-narratives, and may occasionally be heard to remark in passing that Henry David Thoreau solitudinized himself. They rarely conflate or imbricate, and they neither marginalize nor pathologize the Other. They transgress norms whenever possible, and on nice days they like to destabilize a hegemon.

Unfortunately, they must go off to work in a quite different universe, to earn money by teaching in universities. In this secondary world, which some call "real," they constitute a steadily growing force. They are by tradition dedicated proselytizers, like Mormons, and their numbers steadily increase. They are not yet a voting bloc but certainly they constitute a plague in the lives of students and a serious concern to anyone who considers clear language a part of civilized life and regards the university as a pillar of civilization.

The American historian P.N. Limerick depicted them as a major scandal in the *New York Times* eleven years ago: "While we waste our time fighting over ideological conformity in the scholarly world, horrible writing remains a far more important problem." That may overstate the case, but certainly the wretched style of academic theorists amounts to a serious nuisance. It has not become any less oppressive since Limerick wrote those words. In fact, theorists have grown more brazen, even to the point of implying (as we shall see) that bad writing is good for you.

"Have something to say, and say it as clearly as you can," Matthew Arnold ordered. He is not much quoted today. Proponents of critical theory are more likely to quote Jean-Francois Lyotard, when they are not quoting Jacques Derrida or Walter Benjamin or Jacques Lacan. They love quoting; they believe it validates their work by linking it with the European masters they admire. Theorists are even happier, if possible, when introducing to the innocent an obscure and terrifying literary term. Their habit is to make the unknown word appear with magical suddenness, as if from out of nowhere. Typically, they provide only the most cursory explanation.

Heteronormativity provides the perfect example. The OED doesn't know that word, but Dr Janice Stewart of the University of British Columbia does. In the current UBC catalogue she informs potential students of a new course given by the Centre for Cross-Faculty Inquiry in Education – "Queer Theory: Identity, Agency and School(ed) Subjects" – which, she promises, will introduce

> ... the interdisciplinary field of Queer theory and its implications for a critical consideration of pedagogy and the production of subjectivity. Queer theory has generally been mobilized in the service of non-normative sexualities and desires to destabilise and contest the often concealed hegemony of what Michael Warner has termed 'heteronormativity.'

Across North America there are now hundreds of faculties in which language of that kind appears almost routine. It began in philosophy and English departments and then spread, some 15 or 20 years ago, to schools of art and cinema. It has been particularly welcomed in film schools as a way of giving a veneer of scholarship to a field that always teeters on the brink of triviality.

Theorists writing about film, including those visiting from departments such as philosophy and literature, can reassure students, and perhaps deans and provosts, that the subject is truly complex and therefore significant. By making otherwise simple ideas appear difficult if not impossible to understand, they demonstrate the seriousness of film studies.

Last year the *Los Angeles Times* carried a poignant article by David Weddle, a scriptwriter and journalist who graduated in film from the University of Southern California 25 years ago. His daughter recently enrolled in the same school and discovered herself dropped into a nest of writhing theorists. She showed her father an examination paper, which quoted a passage from Kristin Thompson's film theory:

We may define the viewer as a hypothetical entity who responds actively to cues within the film on the basis of automatic perceptual processes and on the basis of experience. Since historical contexts make the protocols of these responses inter-subjective, we may analyze films without resorting to subjectivity.... According to Bordwell, 'The organism constructs a perceptual judgement on the basis of nonconscious inferences.'

A question followed: "What kind of pressure would Metz's description of 'the imaginary signifier' or Baudry's account of the subject in the apparatus put on the ontology and epistemology of film implicit in the above two statements?" Weddle soon found himself stumbling across words such as "diegetic," "heterogeneity," "narratology," "narrativity," "scopophilia," and "syntagmatic." He did not begin to understand what his daughter was studying; and neither, apparently, did she.

Some students find critical theory so intimidating that they assume the fault is theirs if they fail to grasp it. Others will wonder why academics are apparently doing all they can to maintain the greatest possible distance between writer and reader. Students like Weddle's daughter, possibly hoping to make actual films some day, are also astonished to learn that critical theorists believe their own writing to be at least as important as that of artists they are studying, and sometimes more important. Theorists almost automatically superimpose their own concerns on the material they write about, often to the point of implying that filmmakers, painters, etc., exist so that professors can devise theories about them. They foreground (as they would say) the act of theorizing while backgrounding (as they would say) what others might expect to be the principal subject of criticism and study, the art "product."

In the fall, 2003 issue of *Film Criticism*, Christopher D. Morris, the Charles A. Dana Professor of English at Norwich University in Northfield, Vermont, wrote on "The reflexivity of the road film," and in particular Gus Van Sant's 1991 film, *My Own Private Idaho*. After the ritual quoting of key names (Baudrillard, Derrida, Paul de Man)

and key terms ("the simulacrum," "hyperreality," etc.), Morris
dealt with the film and in particular with Mike (the River Phoenix
character), a male prostitute who suffers from narcolepsy. After
delivering a monologue, Mike falls asleep and drops to the ground,
a fall Morris interpreted as essentially an event in film theory:

> Mike's story becomes unstuck when he yields to the call of
> narcolepsy, to the oneiric, to a secondary dream-state within
> the already-acknowledged dream-state of film, a move that
> renounces the search for hermeneutic templates that might
> measure characters' achievement of autonomy, subjectivity,
> or integrity or the extent of a film's deviation from generic or
> ideological norms. For film criticism to become oneiric in this
> sense would mean to replace hermeneutic studies with acts of
> letting-go or creative drift ...

These are sentences that beg to be put out of their misery, yet
they come from the word processor of an English professor. In
that regard they are not unusual. We can now expect to encounter academics who have spent years reading Shakespeare or Jane
Austen yet proudly turn out barbarous prose and encourage young
people to imitate them. It was an English professor, Linda Charnes
of Indiana University, who wrote, in a collection called *Philosophical
Shakespeares* (2000):

> Mass culture is being increasingly 'quilted,' to use Lacan's term,
> by the points de capiton of what I would call the 'apparition-
> al historical.' It is therefore no accident that Hamlet is the
> play to which contemporary culture most frequently returns.
> Hamlet-the-prince has come to stand for the dilemma of
> historicity itself ...

Are they posing, or do they truly believe that their ideas are
best conveyed through writing of this kind? Russell Jacoby, who
wrote *The Last Intellectuals* (1987), has said that academic culture in
the humanities tends to foster the belief that "fractured English,

name dropping, and abstractions guarantee profundity, profession-alisation and subversion."

"Subversion" is a crucial word here. Subverting accepted ideas, most notably imperialistic ideas, provides the urgent moral purpose lying behind much critical theory. Traditional ways of thought having encouraged or permitted the oppression of humanity, critical theory will pierce to its heart and free us all. That's the assumption, at least. But why does this promised freedom involve suffocating readers with coagulated ideas? Why does liberation require that students and other interested readers enter a cage of deadening, frustrating, and infuriating prose?

The Sapir-Whorf Hypothesis, developed in the 1930s by the linguists Edward Sapir and Benjamin Lee Whorf, holds that the language we use will determine how we see the world. As Sapir wrote, "Human beings ... are very much at the mercy of the particular language which has become the medium of expression for their society." Language shapes and limits our perceptions.

Something like this lies behind the prose of theorists in the humanities. They are not oblivious (as some might guess) to the gnarled, ungainly effect of their writing, but they have no interest in "improving" their literary skills. If they are incompetent it's by choice. Moreover, they do not accept the now widespread theory that their style is a way of establishing themselves as a priestly class. Brian Martin, an Australian professor, has called their terminology "secret passwords at the gate of knowledge." Jargon, he thinks, polices the boundaries of disciplines and specialities, keeping out those who have not paid the toll (i.e., learned the language) before crossing the border. Theorists will have none of that; they believe they are the true democrats, delivering (in their fashion) the truth that will set us free.

Over the years they have answered complaints about their writing with little more than sullen silence. Finally they were provoked to action by the campaign of Denis Dutton, editor of *Philosophy and Literature* and of the on-line anthology *Arts & Letters Daily*. Dutton ran a Bad Writing contest through *Philosophy and Literature*, inviting readers to submit samples of "the most egregious examples of

awkward, jargon-clogged academic prose from all over the English-speaking world."

The writers whose prose was thus foregrounded include several
leading theorists, most notably Judith Butler of Berkeley, who
theorizes on the subject of gender. Dutton's winning quotations
were reproduced on-line, holding their authors up to ridicule. In
1999 he also wrote a much-quoted article, "Language Crimes:
A Lesson in How Not to Write, Courtesy of the Professoriate," in
the *Wall Street Journal*.

Last year the theorists finally fought back. Essays by fifteen of
them were brought together in *Just Being Difficult? Academic Writing
in the Public Arena* (2003), edited by Jonathan D. Culler and Kevin
Lamb of Cornell. Called to explain themselves and their peers, they
resort to several strategies. The editors claim to find it puzzling that
people like Dutton simply quote what they call bad writing rather
than explaining why it's bad. Scratching their heads, they wonder
why it appears "not to require explanation or demonstration, as if
all one has to do is quote a sentence and people will instantly recognize how awful it is." In fact, this is the case. As Louis Armstrong
said when asked for a definition of jazz, "There are some people that
if they don't know, you can't tell 'em."

Perhaps, Culler and Lamb say, "bad" simply means "unclear" or
"needlessly obscure." But what about modern poetry and fiction? If
people accept that a poem or a novel can be unclear, why not criticism? They can't see why the allowances for "richness and intrica-
cy" that we make in poetry should not be extended to the work of
theorists. At some point in their intellectual history, these authors
have lost sight of the difference between literature and writing about
literature. While few show even hints of literary talent, they nevertheless demand the tolerance and careful attention that artists win by
their brilliance.

A little more convincingly, contributors to the book argue that so-
called "bad writing" is simply difficult writing that must be difficult
to accomplish its intentions. Judith Butler begins her essay with a
passage that sounds slightly like Gertrude Stein and slightly like a
confession. As with most confessions in print, it turns out to be a

form of self-justification:

> I am wondering how to write this essay. Will I be intelligible
> or not? And if I am intelligible, does that mean that I have
> succeeded? And if I am not quite intelligible, or if I am unin-
> telligible, then will that be a failure of communication? Or
> will it be making a different point?

Her answer to the last question is Yes. She and others in the
book obviously believe that it's for the good of their readers that
they write badly (though they don't accept that word). They are
developing fresh thoughts, which require fresh means of expression.
As the Sapir-Whorf Hypothesis implies, a new way of thinking
requires a new language. So they "defamiliarize" ordinary academic
language, thus awakening their readers to unfamiliar realities.
The unconventional style they have developed calls attention not
only to itself but to the investigations of language that are among
their main purposes.

Alas, critical theory's unconventional style has by now become
conventional and overly familiar. The authors of *Just Being Difficult?*
write in a manner now encrusted with clichés and eroded by over-
use. Once, perhaps, it could lay claim to being a literary strategy for
intellectual revolutionaries; at worst it promised the pleasures of
novelty. Now it is so deeply embedded in the world of culture and
scholarship that its justification as an attention getter has disappeared. But it will not vanish, as many optimists have been predicting for years. We may accurately describe it as an experiment that
failed, but its practitioners now use it with such pleasure and ease
that the world can expect to encounter it for decades to come.

Thomas Carlyle, commenting on Victorian books about Britain's
Puritan heritage, remarked: "The sound of them is not a voice con-
veying knowledge ... of any earthly or heavenly thing; it is a widespread inarticulate slumberous mumblement." Carlyle liked that
sixteenth-century word, "mumblement," and used it at least three
times. It's been out of action for a long time, but no word I know
describes so well the work of the critical theorists.

Newark in Myth and History

Leslie Fiedler, a famously ferocious American literary critic in the middle of the twentieth century, wrote that "To be an American is precisely to imagine a destiny rather than to inherit one; since we have always been, insofar as we are Americans at all, inhabitants of myth rather than history." He must have had that in mind when he reviewed Philip Roth's first book, *Goodbye, Columbus*, published in 1959. Many of the stories are explicitly set in Newark, New Jersey, Roth's hometown and also Fiedler's. In Fiedler's view, Roth was drawing Newark into literature and giving it a sense of reality, a certain mythic density, that it previously lacked.

A city does not truly exist until it appears in the work of an important writer. Newark was Nowhere, USA, and Roth had turned it into Somewhere. Fiedler said he was grateful that he could now name Newark as his birthplace, without embarrassment.

Since then much has happened to Newark, some of it horribly real, some of it on the level of the mythologies Fiedler loved to trace. The 1967 race riot, among the most notorious of that period, wrecked much of the city and left emotional wounds that remain unhealed. Mythologically, the most famous television drama of recent times, *The Sopranos*, installed its protagonist, Tony Soprano, in a Newark suburb and derived much of Tony's professional biography from the career of Richard ("Richie the Boot") Boiardo, for many years the Genovese family's feudal lord in Newark. Meanwhile, Philip Roth, perhaps the most impressive novelist now writing in English, has reimagined Newark again and again, adding flesh layers to local legend.

I'm one of those people who never entertained a single thought about Newark before the 1960s. I still haven't visited it and may never do so. But as a reader of Roth I believe in some literary corner of my mind that I know the place intimately. That's the kind of surprise that appears spontaneously in the lives of readers, creeping up on us as an author leads us into the contents of his imagination.

In this case it turns out to have been an unexpected event in the life of the writer as well. As he learned his craft Roth never imagined himself as the Bard of Newark. In 1950 he left for university when he was barely 17, and he has not lived there since. As he says, "I, myself am surprised I'm so mesmerized by this place, because I left younger than any of my friends. And I never went back." Many friends returned after college and moved to nearby suburbs when Newark itself became unbearable. Roth has lived in New York, Rome, London, and now Western Massachusetts – but never stopped writing about Newark. This is only one of the two ways Roth has been surprised by his own writing. The other has to do with Judaism.

In *Operation Shylock*, published in 1993, he reflects on his ethnic roots. Speaking as the semi-fictional character named Philip Roth, he writes of:

> ... that topic I could not really remember having chosen to
> shadow me like this, from birth to death; the topic whose
> obsessive examination I had always thought I could someday
> leave behind; ... the pervasive, engulfing, wearying topic that
> encapsulated the largest problem and most amazing experience
> of my life and that, despite every honorable attempt to resist its
> spell, appeared to be the irrational power that had run away
> with my life – and, from the sound of things, not mine alone ...
> that topic called the Jews.

Perhaps he took such a firm grip on this subject because he realized that his fellow Jews provided the richest material given to him by his life. There was another factor, however, more specific to his era. History was leading Roth and everyone else away from the idea of the universal and toward the particular. What we now call multiculturalism (though that was hardly even a word when Roth started out) was becoming a central part of North American thought.

More general historic themes have followed him through his career. He has never written historical novels, but in book after book he has taken pains to work through varieties of historic experiences – immigration, radicalism in the 1930s and the 1960s, evolving male-female relations, the Middle East, and literature itself.

At times he has toyed with counter-history, speculating on the way things might have worked out if only a few details were changed. In his 1979 novel, *The Ghost Writer*, he raises the possibility that Anne Frank survived the Holocaust and turned up in the life of an American writer very much like Bernard Malamud. And earlier than that, in 1973, he wrote a piece, part story and part essay, called "'I Always Wanted You to Admire My Fasting'; or, Looking at Kafka."

In Roth's imagining, Franz Kafka has not only lived into the 1940s but has escaped from Europe and found a job teaching Hebrew school at the Schley Street Synagogue in Newark. Roth's narrator, one of Kafka's students, tells us that his aunt Rhoda feels attracted to Kafka's "big, sad eyes." They go to a movie, and the narrator's family offers friendship to the strange man from Prague. But the relationship doesn't take flight. More important, Kafka's stories have not survived, and he dies unknown, his only obituary a brief note in a Newark paper. Roth has also found himself examining history as a force that suddenly overwhelms and destroys individuals who believe they have found a safe harbour for their lives.

Anyone who studies the currents of the last century, especially a Jew, carries around the knowledge of what happened to the German and Austrian Jews who played a large and vigorous part in the lives of their countries until they were told that they were not only unwanted but that their governments were planning to kill them. For those victims, history exploded, in a way that almost no one could have predicted.

Roth refers in *Operation Shylock* to a famous individual case of someone destroyed in a sudden random sweep of history's sword: Leon Klinghoffer, the American Jewish appliance manufacturer, thrown over the side of the *Achille Lauro* cruise ship in his wheelchair on October 8, 1985. It was an act of wanton murder, by PLO terrorists, as cruel as it was abrupt. Roth describes it: "An ordinary person who purely by accident gets caught in the historical struggle. A life annotated by history in the last place you expect history to intervene. On a cruise, which is out of history in every way."

Toward the end of the twentieth century Roth developed three characters who are destroyed by a bizarre eruption of history in their midst. At the heart of *American Pastoral* (1997), *I Married a Communist* (1998), and *The Human Stain* (2000), historic changes ambush individuals and leave their lives in ruins. As a result, Roth has attracted the attention of a professional historian, Michael Kimmage of the Catholic University of America. Kimmage has written a shrewd, imaginative, and sympathetic book, *In History's Grip: Philip Roth's Newark Trilogy* (2012).

American Pastoral is the most ambitious of the Roth trilogy and the one most often called a masterpiece, the book in which he expands his original subject, the Newark Jews, until they represent all of immigrant America and then, at certain moments, all of America. It attracted particular attention because it arrived in Roth's 65th year, at a time when we might have expected him to ease into semiretirement, having already produced a substantial shelf of remarkable books. Of course we didn't know that there would be two more impressive novels in the next two years and then at least seven more titles in the twenty-first century. As Kimmage says, the books in the trilogy are tied together in several ways. In each of them Roth uses the same narrator, Nathan Zuckerman, who has often played that role in other Roth books: Zuckerman is a framing device, an extra author, providing distance from the story while reminding us, from time to time, that this is a work of fiction, even though at times it's piercingly convincing.

In the grammar of these three novels, as Kimmage writes, "Newark is the subject of the sentence, and the trilogy's protagonists are its direct objects, set in motion by the moving city." It is easy enough to leave Newark physically; but leaving it spiritually and mythologically is far more difficult and in many cases impossible. Each of the protagonists ends up experiencing history as a trauma. It arrives in the form of enraged left-wing radicals or a vindictive congressional committee or a wave of political correctness that has descended, within the universities, into raw meanness.

The three individuals in these novels all leave Newark to recreate themselves and build lives that do not reflect their actual histories. They move to an affluent old community in a New Jersey suburb, or Manhattan, or Western Massachusetts. They marry outside their city and their clan. They are adventurous, but they are blindsided by the history they cannot know, the history through which they are living – as Roth says, "the present moment, the common lot, the current

mood, the mind of one's country, the stranglehold of history that
is one's own time." We assume we know our own time because we
spend much of our lives examining and discussing it; but it is only in
retrospect that we can truly begin to understand it.

American Pastoral represents Roth's revised view of the 1960s. He
drew strength from the liberationist ethos of that era; in *Portnoy's
Complaint*, published in 1969, he borrows from the manic spritzing
monologues of Lenny Bruce, who gave 1960s radicalism its jagged,
intransigent voice. Roth swam in the broth of anarchy that Bruce
cooked up. In that era he naturally sympathized with the students
opposing the Vietnam war, but in *American Pastoral* both the jokes
and the banal leftist rhetoric have withered. Violent radicalism
becomes the eruption that destroys the family of Seymour ("the
Swede") Levov when his unhappy, stuttering, 16-year-old daughter,
Merry, accidentally kills an innocent man while bombing their
local post office in the wealthy suburb of Old Rimrock, New Jersey.
Reviewers saw this as Roth's American version of The Book of Job:
Levov, who had achieved everything an American might desire, is
brought low. But God is not the source of his downfall; history is the
calamity from which he cannot escape.

In *I Married a Communist* Ira Ringold is a Newark Jew who becomes
a star on national radio and a well-connected cultural communist,
even a friend of Paul Robeson. He escapes both poverty and Newark
by marrying a wealthy star from the silent movies, Eve Frame. The
history that destroys Ringold is represented by McCarthyism's arbitrary, irresponsible denunciations of mostly ineffective leftists; Ira is
driven mad by the unexpected vehemence of his new enemies.

The Human Stain focuses on two of the central themes of American
culture, the anxiety and fury surrounding ethnicity and what Roth
calls "The drama that underlies America's story, the high drama
that is upping and leaving – and the energy and cruelty that rapturous drive demands." Coleman Silk makes an especially radical break
from his past: born with whitish skin in a black family, he decides
to "pass" for white rather than accept the fate that appears to be
prepared for him. This is a truly American idea. He embraces
"The passionate struggle for singularity," so that his fate will be

determined "not by the ignorant, hate-filled intentions of a hostile world but, to whatever degree humanly possible, by his own resolve." As a white man, calling himself Jewish, he becomes a professor of classics at a small college in Massachusetts. He's escaped. But he's brought down by a force that he could never have seen coming – the crazy fad of political correctness that came to dominate all talk of race in American university life. In a classroom Silk speaks a few words that are intentionally misinterpreted as anti-black. His fellow teachers fail to support him, and his downfall is swift.

More than half a century ago Lionel Trilling, the great critic, argued that American literature defines itself by its way of transcending the social fact and concentrating upon the individual. Typically, it represents society and ordinary life as problems posed, problems to be dealt with. *Huckleberry Finn, An American Tragedy, The Catcher in the Rye* are three among many examples. But Roth, in the Newark trilogy, offers three protagonists who see the limitations in their surroundings, make the most strenuous efforts to escape from them, and in the end find themselves defeated by events neither they nor anyone else could have anticipated. They have set out to conquer society rather than letting it conquer them; for a long time each of them seems to have pulled it off. Then they discover that society has reached out, reclaimed, and defeated them. In the Newark trilogy we watch the great American comic novelist of our time prove he is also a master of tragedy.

Remorse in Dickens, Remorse in Me

A truly great book should be read in youth, again in maturity and once more in old age, as a fine building should be seen by morning light, at noon and by moonlight.
—ROBERTSON DAVIES

In grade nine at Malvern Collegiate in Toronto, in the autumn of 1945, I encountered what has ever since seemed to me the perfect novel for a 13-year-old and a fine novel for anyone else, *Great Expectations*. It was my first serious novel by Charles Dickens. In its pages I discovered all the crucial themes that established him as the greatest of English novelists and our most articulate witness to Victorian England, that place and time from which so much of the modern world (including modern Canada) sprang.

But on the way to uncovering this material we young readers discovered more familiar motifs. Today we would say that Dickens drew heavily on genre conventions. Situations that were familiar to us from children's stories (and developed by the early comic books for our generation) constitute much of the plot.

Philip Pirrip, known mostly as Pip, the orphan who serves as both hero and narrator, is seven years old when he encounters a monster in the book's opening scene. The atmosphere echoes Gothic fiction. Pip is visiting the graveyard where his parents and his five siblings are buried, on the edge of ominous marshes, near the gallows where criminals are hanged. From out of nowhere a rough-voiced man speaks, seizes Pip, turns him upside down to empty his pockets, and threatens him with a grisly death unless he obtains what the man needs desperately – food ("wittles") and a file.

To Pip his assailant seems a monster, but a monster he recalls in horrifying detail:

> *A fearful man, all in coarse grey, with a great iron on his leg. A man with no hat, and with broken shoes, and with an old rag tied round his head. A man who limped, and shivered, and glared and growled; and whose teeth chattered in his head as he seized me by the chin.*

The language of Dickens has a way of turning a character from a nightmare into something vividly real. He used it well when he shaped the grotesque opening of Great Expectations.

The man on the marshes is Abel Magwitch, who will play a large part in the novel; in fact, he'll eventually turn into a kind of fairy godfather, sending money all the way from Australia to smooth Pip's way through life. At this point Pip knows only that he's an escaped convict anxious to be freed from his chains. Terrorized, Pip steals food and a file from the blacksmith's shop run by his brother-in-law, Joe Gargery, knowing it is wrong to steal but afraid to do otherwise. Nevertheless, Magwitch is recaptured, and Pip's crime remains undiscovered.

The fairy-story elements persist. Pip meets a beautiful girl, Estella, a princess who is under the thrall of an ogre, a rich and grotesque old woman, Miss Havisham. It is clearly Pip's duty, for her sake and his own, to rescue Estella from the clutches of this witch. But what power does he possess? He seems destined to live in poverty as an apprentice to Joe, perhaps someday succeeding him at the forge.

Dickens solves this problem by having a lawyer, Mr Jaggers, arrive with startling news: a patron, whose name must remain unknown, wishes to provide a large sum of money so that Pip can be properly educated and turned into a gentleman. Who can this anonymous philanthropist be?

I cherish our schoolroom discussions of this question because it was a rare occasion, possibly even the only occasion, when I had a chance to feel smarter than my best friend in that era, Glenn Gould. He was the brightest school kid I ever met, as well as a musical genius. When we were given our geometry book many of us found it challenging and took most of the school year to work our way through it. Glenn, on the other hand, mastered the whole thing in six or eight weeks, without stumbling once.

But when it came to Great Expectations, I was just a little brighter. Pip believed the secret philanthropist must be Miss Havisham. I decided it was Magwitch. Glenn hadn't thought of that but agreed it was likely true. "You must have read the ending first," he said. I truthfully testified that I was no farther along than anyone else in the class. I had just figured it out. So far as I can recall, that was my last intellectual victory over Glenn.

Patricia Meyer Spacks, in her book *On Rereading* (2011), says that "The sense of having it both ways, of preserving the joy that is the object of nostalgia while possessing new powers of understanding, makes the rereading of treasures from long ago especially satisfying." Rereading can break open new meanings in an old book and multiply its implications. We always discover there is more to it than we at first noticed.

We know more than we knew then, and one thing we know more about is our own lives. Reading a book we loved long ago sets up a dialogue between our younger and older selves, or, if we follow the Davies three-part formula, we set up a conversation among our young self, our middle-aged self, and our old self. We reread ourselves while rereading a text. Sometimes the text judges us. But in this case we are first asked to judge Pip.

He's a good-hearted boy, but he's swamped emotionally by two unprecedented events, the appearance of Estella and the prospect of a new life as a gentleman. Proud, beautiful Estella arouses his dreams of romance while simultaneously dashing them. "You must know," she says, "that I have no heart." Miss Havisham, abandoned on her wedding day, hates all males and has taught Estella to share her hatred. But when Pip's unknown patron proposes to make him a gentleman, he assumes that will change everything.

A gentleman, it is understood, can have anything he wants. Transformed, Pip will deserve and thus win Estella. This foolish vanity leads him into an unearned sense of pride. When he's acquired some sense of language and propriety, his new status as a gentleman overcomes his innate goodness. Dickens uses this transformation to satirize and condemn the system of money and class governing England. But he probably touched more of his readers (and, at a guess, himself) by describing through Pip's life the moral failures of those whose pride or simple forgetfulness makes them disloyal to the people who have been close to them.

At the beginning we know that Joe Gargery is Pip's best friend, companion, and model – "ever the best of friends," as Joe always says. Pip in boyhood agrees. But Pip the gentleman finds him an embarrassment. When Joe comes for a visit, his clothes, his words, and his awkwardness don't suit Pip's new lodging and Pip's new friends. Joe sees the truth and abruptly ends his visit. But he knows this is simply the way it goes: "Pip, dear old chap, life is made of ever so many partings welded together."

Pip's shame over this incident, and his later avoidance of Joe, becomes part of his maturing. It is only when he regrets the crimes of his own heart that he becomes his true self. Remorse is the key to his eventual maturity and largeness of spirit. But Joe as a moral issue is relatively simple beside Magwitch. He shows up, once more a fugitive from justice, once more wanting Pip's help. "Look'ee here, Pip. I'm your second father. You're my son ... I've put away money, only for you to spend." The help he needs is difficult and dangerous, but Pip does his best.

The advice of Davies makes the greatest sense when we have accumulated enough years to value the past. At some point we see the profound silliness of people who say "Forget the past, move on." It is only when we learn to embrace the past, when we set aside that vacuous line, Je ne regrette rien, and admit to ourselves that there is much to regret – only then can we take Pip's moral evolution to heart.

An innocent 13-year-old reader, as I was when first approaching this book, blundering hastily through it in grade nine, mainly anxious to know how it comes out, could only imagine the depths of Pip's remorse. At that stage we can't feel the meaning of his crime because we have never committed it, or at most have done so in such a casual way that it had little meaning. Remorse needs to marinate for a while before it has any commendable effect on our behaviour. I needed my second reading, in middle age, to understand what Dickens said about the banalities and ugliness of class. I needed my third reading, in old age, to grasp why I have always had such strong positive feelings for Pip: in my way I've shared his crimes, and learned to regret them. I've dropped friends out of impatience or annoyance or for my own convenience. My hope is that my experience of remorse (with, no doubt, some help from Pip and similarly self-searching fictional characters) has improved me.

The ending of *Great Expectations* is itself one of the great curiosities in Dickens' career and one I've only understood during my third reading.

Dickens originally shaped the ending as a brief, precise dismissal of the two might-have-been lovers whose relationship readers had been wondering about for many chapters. As Dickens saw it there was no future for Pip and Estella; there had been too many hard words, and too much disappointment. So it ended with them permanently separated, the greatest of Pip's expectations unfulfilled.

Strangely (at least it seems strange today), it was Edward Bulwer-Lytton, a good friend of Dickens, who read the completed manuscript and suggested a fundamental change. He urged that something resembling a happy ending be substituted. Bulwer-Lytton's great success was *The Last Days of Pompeii* (1834), but today he's best remembered for writing what many consider the worst of all openings of a novel, the passage that begins the book he entitled *Paul Clifford* (1830): "It was a dark and stormy night ..."

Even so, Dickens respected him and took his advice seriously. How did Bulwer-Lytton put the case (as Mr Jaggers would say) that Dickens should move from pessimism to optimism? Biographers can't tell us, but we can guess.

He saw what Dickens didn't, that a happy resolution between Pip and Estella, their total reconciliation after a long parting, was the ending toward which the whole story was pointing. The audience would demand it.

Dickens apparently agreed, but the final printed version turned out to be vague, a little grudging, not quite an affirmation of Pip-Estella love. "I saw no shadow of another parting from her," Pip tells us. But it's clear from what Estella says that she's not at all sure they have a future together. It was as if Dickens were hinting that in the nonexistent post-book future, his two frustrated lovers would find a way to wreck their relationship, and the original ending he had written would be proven the right one after all.

How It All Comes Out: The Obit Writer Reluctantly Thinks of Death

S
ad and unsettling news arrived by phone early on the morning of December 2, 1966: Ralph Allen, one of the best journalists of his time, a hero for me when I was a teenager and later a model of excellence in my profession, had died unexpectedly, at age 53. The call was a request that I write about him for the *Toronto Star*, where I worked for eight years in the 1960s and where Allen was managing editor at his death.

I took a long breath and let it out slowly. Fifty-three! That was outrageous. Those of us who admired his work and benefited from his kindness were bitterly disappointed, believing we were entitled to enjoy him for another 20 years. Maybe, with luck, more.

Still, I had another reaction, perhaps surprising, at almost the same moment. I was glad to have the chance to write an obituary tribute to him. I wasn't even intimidated by the fact that the piece had to be produced in the next two hours. In fact, I remember experiencing a kind of pleasure as I wrote it.

Writing for me usually involves pleasure, always shaded by performance anxiety, but in those ancient days obituaries offered unique satisfaction. This might be classified as a minor perversity, perhaps what the French call a déformation professionnelle (so much more dignified than "mental conditioning caused by one's job"), but for some reason writing an obituary of a notable person seemed to me, for many years, a desirable assignment. Mastering this minor journalistic art, the printed gesture of farewell, seemed important to me. And I tended to believe that no one did it better, provided the subject was someone I had thought about, ideally over a long time.

When I was writing for *The Globe and Mail* in the 1990s an editor, noting the willingness with which I took on the Harold Town and Northrop Frye obits, jokingly described me as "the angel of death." But those were two people whose lives, long familiar to me, deserved whatever elegance I could offer them.

At various times, in various publications, I wrote a final salute (usually one of many final salutes) to Ernest Hemingway and A.Y. Jackson, Lionel Trilling and George Grant, Adlai Stevenson and Roland Barthes. It grew into my form of mourning, my way of carving a small monument. Doing it right became crucial.

I wrote also about a few people close to me, in particular two close friends who were also distinguished journalists of my own generation, Barbara Frum and Peter Gzowski. I cried over them, then and later, and miss them still. Yet I thought it important to write about them. When it was over, I was glad I did. Glenn Gould, the lovable genius whose boyhood I shared, evoked a different kind of mourning. At age 50 I found myself trying to recall the childhood I had always classified as boring and was only beginning to appreciate for its good qualities.

People often say they begin to feel old the first time they realize that policemen look young. Later they have the same uncomfortable feelings about aging when they encounter increasingly juvenile-looking doctors, dentists, bank clerks, and prime ministers. I've been able, so far as I know, to keep those observations in check, as minor amusements. My own serious proof of age, the clear and brutal sign that my years were affecting me emotionally as well as physically, was the slow realization that the obituary, as a form of literary expression, was losing its charm.

I've never stopped writing obits and may write another of them tomorrow. It's often a duty, to one's editors or to posterity or to both. But at some point, perhaps between Billy Wilder's death in 2002 and Marlon Brando's in 2004, it became clear that my enthusiasm was waning.

What could that mean? Was it possible that death, which I had decided long ago to regard with insouciance as no more than the final (though often bungled) act in the human comedy, was having its way, conducting a sneak attack on my unconscious? Was I letting the death of someone else, the ending of his or her story, cast a shadow over my own life?

In 2004, some months before Brando's death (though no connection is exactly provable) my heart developed an atrial flutter. This has on three occasions required cardioversion, a mild electric shock that dramatically lifts me an inch or so off the hospital bed but serves as a sharp warning to my atria that they are to behave. Miraculously, they obey.

Then, three years ago, I had a stroke. It was a "minor" stroke even if it seemed relatively major to the patient and his family. In the end I more or less dodged the bullet, thanks to timely drilling by professional therapists and my zealous and therapy-talented wife. After six weeks of intense fatigue, I recovered, with only a few pieces of evidence left at the scene to prove that something had happened. My voice was permanently changed from fairly sharp and emphatic to faint, woolly, and husky. I lost some conversational fluency and some of my automatic word-finding ability. I occasionally misplaced words. In conversation I still sometimes stumble about, searching, while a word I need eludes me, even a word like "treadmill." Playing *Balderdash* with friends, I couldn't find "abacus," no matter how hard I knitted my brow. Tragically, I lost the game. But my memory of events remained true, so far as I can determine.

It seems clear that, one way and another, the stroke altered my feelings about age. Cicero tells us that old age, aside from its three most obvious ill effects (it limits what we can do, weakens our bodies, and spoils many forms of enjoyment), has a fourth way of making us unhappy – "It stands not far from death." That seems to be the problem.

I suppose I should state my age. How old am I? I share with most middle-aged people the ability to say where I was when John Kennedy was shot (in a restaurant called L'Europe on Bloor Street West in Toronto, lunching with my friend and *Maclean's* magazine colleague, Jack Batten). But that's just the beginning. Even if we limit ourselves to public affairs and set aside for another time the births of my four offspring, I can tunnel surprisingly deep into my memories of notable events.

I remember exactly what I felt in 1957 when, at an election-night party with other journalists, I realized that John Diefenbaker and the Conservatives were bringing down Louis St. Laurent's Liberal government, which till then seemed likely to be eternal. (I felt deep revulsion and horror, and when Diefenbaker became prime minister he did everything possible to justify my worst forebodings.) I know within a couple of blocks the location of the restaurant where, taking a break from my 1945 summer job as a Canadian Pacific Telegraphs bicycle courier, I ate lunch while reading in the *Toronto Star* that the Americans had dropped an atomic bomb on Hiroshima. I celebrated V-J Day, as I had celebrated V-E Day the previous spring, by standing in a crowd and looking at other people standing in the crowd.

In June 1944, waiting behind Williamson Road Public School for the start of the class day, I discussed with a friend the landing of the Allied troops on the beach in Normandy. I can't recall hearing George VI give his address to the world in 1939, the one that provides the climax for The King's Speech, but I remember the adults in our house talking about how it demonstrated that he had improved his speaking ability. I was three weeks short of my fourth birthday when George V died, in 1936, but an aural memory stays with me: for some reason I didn't understand, the radio played unusual music (hymns, presumably) all day long.

Put it another way: I am so old that I have protégés who are has-beens. It is unavoidable that if one is born in February 1932, one had one's seventy-ninth birthday this past winter and on that day realized that one was just 365 days away from being an octogenarian. Not to put too fine a point on it, what we have here is an old person. I refuse to retire (it is said to be a major cause of death) and insist I will continue to practice journalism as long as there are journals (or, if necessary, blogs) that will carry my words. A student journalist at Ryerson University e-mailed me with a query: "How long do you plan to write for the *National Post* ?" I answered: "Till they tell me to stop."

This exchange reminded me that, at some moment, the status of every senior citizen changes. If the world hasn't heard of someone for a while, the world assumes he or she is dead. Worse, they may know you are very much alive and wonder why. Here we approach a fundamental contradiction in the desires and assumptions of our society. We agree to do all that's humanly possible to keep everyone alive indefinitely, but we can't think what they should do with themselves. Among those who have picked up a fragment of anthropology there's a feeling, expressed only obliquely, that there is a time when the decent thing is to move yourself to a convenient ice floe.

It's embarrassing to realize that personal longevity plays a major role in my thoughts. It now surpasses public debt, the future of the

Liberal Party, and even the question of paying schoolteachers according to merit. Scanning the death notices, I look first at the age of the newly dead, obviously reflecting a form of competition I would have considered crass and selfish only a decade ago. This indicates I want more years.

But why? Morley Callaghan, at my age, was clearly not yearning for more. At his 80th birthday party, in 1983, a young woman sitting at his table said she would like to be 80. "No," he said, "you want to live to eighty, you don't want to be eighty." I have known old people, quite a few of them, who were anxious to go.

David Murdock, an American billionaire who is now a robust 87, holds the opposite view. According to a recent story in the New York Times, he plans to live to 125 and believes that his fanatically careful eating habits (his smoothies contain pulverized banana peels and ground-up orange rinds) will take him to this unusual plateau. A journalist interviewing him wanted to know why he was so committed to this odds-defying project. It appears that he wants to do it to prove it can be done. He hopes his record-breaking life will demonstrate to the world the benefits of his theories about nutrition.

That's perhaps an egotistical idea, but it's not ignoble. What's my excuse? Reading about Murdock, I wondered why, as my end draws inexorably nearer, I do pretty well all I can to stretch my life. With the support of the federal and provincial governments, I have enough doctors looking after me to staff a small hospital. I think of them as my medical team, an elite coterie of first-class professionals, though most of them have never met the others. They are united mainly by their joint appearances in my appointment book, the making of medical appointments having become one of my main preoccupations.

What is the purpose of all this costly effort? We all believe – or, rather, say we believe – in the sacredness of human life; it follows that individuals naturally think their own lives, being sacred, should be extended as far as possible. But this explanation won't survive two minutes of serious thought. Our civilization thinks nothing of driving cars faster than anyone could justify on grounds of need, knowing that every day on our continent speed kills people. "Respect for life" is a slogan, nothing else.

My reason for wanting more years is curiosity, the reigning impulse of my life, the source of my happiness in work and in private life. In the 1960s a woman in my social and professional circle died suddenly, at the age of 34. We were all devastated. A friend of hers, and mine, said: "I hope she didn't know she was dying. She would have been so angry, not to be able to know what happened to all of us. Not ever knowing how it all came out."

That was said in the haste of grief and of course made no sense. No one ever knows how things come out because things don't stop. If we imagine that there are various billboards recording history in terms of virtue or wealth or evil, we must also imagine that their numbers never stop changing. But this doesn't diminish curiosity. I accept the fact that I won't know what my now five-year-old grandson will study in university, but I'm anxious to see more of his boyhood. I want to follow the life journeys of my wife and my four children; every one of them has surprised and delighted me, and naturally I want more. The same goes for my siblings, nieces, nephews, and friends. They are puzzles, to some extent, puzzles I'll never solve but want, so far as I can, to consider further.

I came rather late to the digitalized world, around 1992, and of course (like all geezers) managed it only with the help of offspring. But once I arrived there I found its pleasures abundant. It brought into my life the two great inventions of the twenty-first century. One is my iPod, which holds hundreds of jazz performances, symphonies, lectures, and broadcasts in a plastic wafer that fits in my shirt pocket. The other is my Kindle, which contains scores of books in a package no bigger than a medium-sized paperback. As I said in a letter to one of my daughters recently – if I had died 10 years ago, and missed both iPod and Kindle, I would have been seriously annoyed.

In certain ways communications technology has made this a more amusing world than I ever expected to know. On the other hand, the "real world" remains appalling. Cruelty and chaos are everywhere. Yesterday my beautiful little iPod read me the BBC news as I walked to my first medical appointment of the day, the one where I give a sample of my blood and a lab determines whether my drugs have thinned it sufficiently to prevent (all other functions going well) another stroke. What the BBC told me yesterday, on this occasion about chaos and cruelty in the Middle East and Africa, sadly confirmed the one truth I know about how it all comes out.

Once more, as W.H. Auden wrote in his most famous poem, "our world in stupor lies, beleaguered by negation and despair." That was in "September 1, 1939." Horrible as it seems, despite all our efforts, the tone of human life, on much of the planet, is as it was 72 years ago. What, then, can we do as we live out our lives? Follow Auden and, so far as we are able, "Show an affirming flame."

ACKNOWLEDGEMENTS

I had the great good luck of being a regular writer for that excellent magazine, the *Queen's Quarterly*. They ran 41 of my essays over the last decade or so, and 28 of those pieces make up the bulk of this book. Whatever is good about them is partly the work of good editing – by the main editor, Boris Castel, and his colleagues, Steve Anderson and Joan Harcourt. Over the years I have had good reason to appreciate their attentive intelligence.

My agent, Beverley Slopen, has been tireless and persistent over the decades I have known and worked with her; this book provides a happy chance to renew our connection. My daughter, Margaret Fulford, chief librarian at University College in the University of Toronto, used her skills to organize the manuscript. With my son James Fulford, they updated and enriched my web page: www.robert.fulford.com

Bryan Gee's talents as a designer will be evident from the cover to the final page. Ian Brown has provided a typically articulate foreword, for which I'm grateful. Dean Baxendale, of Optimum Publishing, has become our welcoming and enthusiastic publisher.

RF

ABOUT THE AUTHOR

Robert Fulford became interested in journalism at an early age. Born in Ottawa in 1932, he learned about storytelling from his mother Frances (Blount) Fulford, the daughter of a printer and granddaughter of a newspaper editor (Edward Clissold of the *London Advertiser*). He learned about journalism from his father A.E. ("Ab") Fulford, an editor and reporter at the Canadian Press who covered the Dionne quintuplets and the 1939 royal tour of Canada. Today many of Frances and Ab Fulford's descendants work in journalism or related fields. Growing up in Toronto's Beach district, Robert was also aware that in 1885 his great-aunt Theresa (Fulford) Delaney had co-authored a book, *Two Months in the Camp of Big Bear*.

By age 16 Robert Fulford was already reporting on high school sports and producing a weekly teen radio show for CHUM; at age 18 (in 1950), he became a *Globe and Mail* reporter. Fulford has had a rich and varied career as a print journalist, broadcaster, and author. In the 1950s and '60s he worked as an editor at *Maclean's* and other magazines, wrote a daily column about books and art for the *Toronto Star* and hosted a weekly CBC radio show. He was the editor of *Saturday Night* magazine from 1968 to 1987, and he co-hosted the TVOntario program *Realities* from 1982 to 1989. He had a weekly *Globe and Mail* column from 1992 to 1999 and became a *National Post* columnist in 1999. His articles have appeared in over 60 magazines and newspapers.

Robert Fulford's books include *This Was Expo* (1968), *Crisis at the Victory Burlesk: Culture, Politics & Other Diversions* (1968), *Marshall Delaney at the Movies: The Contemporary World As Seen On Film* (1974), *Best Seat in the House: Memoirs of a Lucky Man* (1988), *Accidental City: The Transformation of Toronto* (1995) and *The Triumph of Narrative: Storytelling in the Age of Mass Culture* (1999).

Fulford has received 17 National Magazine Awards and five honorary degrees. Married to journalist and author Geraldine Sherman, he has four children and two grandchildren.

For more about Robert Fulford, visit www.robertfulford.com.